Cakes & Desserts

Everyday Cookbook

Publisher and Creative Director: Nick Wells
Art Director: Mike Spender
Project Editor: Cat Emslie
Editorial Planning: Rosanna Singler, Christian Anthony and Victoria Lyle
Layout Design: Mike Spender, Colin Rudderham andVanessa Green
Digital Design and Production: Chris Herbert and Claire Walker

09 11 10 08

1 3 5 7 9 10 8 6 4 2

This edition first published in 2008 by
STAR FIRE
Crabtree Hall, Crabtree Lane,
Fulham, London, SW6 6TY
United Kingdom

www.star-fire.co.uk

STAR FIRE is part of The Foundry Creative Media Company Limited

ISBN 978-1-84786-397-3

The CIP record for this book is available from the British Library.

Printed in China

Authors: Catherine Atkinson, Juliet Barker, Gina Steer, Vicki Smallwood,
Carol Tennant, Mari Mererid Williams, Elizabeth Wolf-Cohen and Simone Wright
Editorial (original edition): Sara Goulding and Sara Robson
Photography: Colin Bowling, Paul Forrester and Stephen Brayne
Home Economists and Stylists: Jacqueline Bellefontaine,
Mandy Phipps, Vicki Smallwood and Penny Stephens

All props supplied by Barbara Stewart at Surfaces

NOTES
All eggs are large, and all fruit and vegetables are medium, unless otherwise stated.
Recipes using uncooked eggs should be avoided by infants,
the elderly, pregnant women and anyone suffering from an illness.

Contents

Everyday Cakes

Cakes for Special Occasions

Desserts

Cleanliness in the Kitchen

It is well worth remembering that many foods can carry some form of bacteria. In most cases, the worst it will lead to is a bout of food poisoning or gastroenteritis, although for certain groups this can be more serious—the risk can be reduced or eliminated by good food hygiene and proper cooking.

Do not buy food that is past its sell-by date, and do not consume food that is past its use-by date. When buying food, use your eyes and nose. If the food looks tired, limp, or discolored, or it has a rank, acrid, or simply bad smell, do not buy or eat it under any circumstances.

Be sure to take special care when preparing raw meat and fish. A separate chopping board should be used for each; wash the knife, board, and your hands thoroughly before handling or preparing any other food.

Regularly clean, defrost, and clear out the refrigerator and freezer—it is worth checking the packaging to see exactly how long each product is safe to freeze.

Avoid handling food if suffering from an upset stomach, since bacteria can be passed through food preparation.

Dishtowels must be washed and changed regularly. Ideally, use paper towels, which can be thrown out after use. Dishtowels should be left to soak in bleach, then washed in hot water in a washing machine.

Keep the hands, cooking utensils, and food preparation surfaces clean, and do not allow pets to climb on to any work surfaces.

Buying

Avoid bulk buying where possible, especially fresh produce such as meat, poultry, fish, fruit, and vegetables. Fresh foods lose their nutritional value rapidly, so buying a little at a time minimizes loss of nutrients. It also eliminates a packed refrigerator, which reduces the effectiveness of the refrigeration process.

When buying prepackaged goods such as cans or cartons of cream and yogurts, check that the packaging is intact and not damaged or pierced. Cans should not be dented, pierced, or rusty. Check the sell-by dates even for cans and packs of dry ingredients such as flour and rice. Store fresh foods in the refrigerator as soon as possible—not in the car or office.

When buying frozen foods, ensure that they are not heavily iced on the outside and the contents feel completely frozen. Make sure that the frozen foods have been stored in the cabinet at the correct storage level and the temperature is below 0°F. Pack in cool bags to transport home, and place in the freezer as soon as possible after purchase.

Preparation

Make sure that all work surfaces and utensils are clean and dry. Hygiene should be given priority at all times. Separate chopping boards should be used for raw and cooked meats, fish, and vegetables. Currently, a variety of good-quality plastic boards come in various designs and colors. This makes differentiating easier, and the plastic has the added hygienic advantage of being washable at high temperatures in the dishwasher. If using the board for fish, first wash in cold water, then in hot to prevent odor. Also, remember that knives and utensils should always be thoroughly cleaned after use.

When cooking, be particularly careful to keep cooked and raw food separate to avoid any contamination. It is worth washing all fruits and vegetables regardless of whether they are going to be eaten raw or lightly cooked. This rule should apply even to prewashed herbs and salads.

Do not reheat food more than once. If using a microwave, always check that the food is piping hot all the way through. (The food should reach 160°F, and needs to be cooked at that temperature for at least three minutes to ensure that all bacteria are killed.)

All poultry must be thoroughly thawed before using. Remove the food to be thawed from the freezer and place in a shallow dish to contain the juices. Leave the food in the refrigerator until it is completely thawed. A 3-lb whole chicken will take about 26–30 hours to thaw. To speed up the process, immerse the chicken in cold water. However, make sure that the water is changed regularly. When the joints can move freely and no ice crystals remain in the cavity, the bird is completely thawed.

Once thawed, remove the wrapper and pat the chicken dry. Place the chicken in a shallow dish, cover lightly, and store as close to the base of the refrigerator as possible. The chicken should be cooked as soon as possible.

Some foods can be cooked from frozen, including many prepacked foods such as soups, sauces, casseroles, and breads. Where applicable, follow the manufacturers' directions.

Vegetables and fruits can also be cooked from frozen, but meats and fish should be thawed first. The only time food can be refrozen is when the food has been thoroughly thawed, then cooked. Once the food has cooled, then it can be frozen again. On such occasions the food can only be stored for one month.

All poultry and game (except for duck) must be cooked thoroughly. When cooked, the juices will run clear on the thickest part of the bird—the best area to try is usually the thigh. Other meats, like ground meat and pork, should be cooked all the way through. Fish should turn opaque, be firm in texture, and break easily into large flakes.

When cooking leftovers, make sure they are reheated until piping hot and

that any sauce or soup reaches boiling point first.

Storing, Refrigerating, and Freezing

Meat, poultry, fish, seafood, and dairy products should all be refrigerated. The temperature of the refrigerator should be between 34–41°F while the freezer temperature should not rise above 0°F. To ensure the optimum refrigerator and freezer temperature, avoid leaving the door open for a long time. Try not to overstock the refrigerator, since this reduces the airflow inside and reduces the effectiveness of cooling the food within.

When refrigerating cooked food, let it cool down quickly and completely before refrigerating. Hot food will raise the temperature of the refrigerator and possibly affect or spoil other food stored inside.

Food within the refrigerator and freezer should always be covered. Raw and cooked food should be stored in separate parts of the refrigerator. Cooked food should be kept on the top shelves of the refrigerator, while raw meat, poultry, and fish should be placed on bottom shelves to avoid drips and cross-contamination. It is recommended that eggs should be refrigerated in order to maintain their freshness and shelf life.

Take care that frozen foods are not stored in the freezer for too long. Blanched vegetables can be stored for one month; beef, lamb, poultry, and pork for six months; and unblanched vegetables and fruits in syrup for a year. Oily fish and sausages should be stored for three months. Dairy products can last four to six months, while cakes and pastries should be kept in the freezer for three to six months.

High Risk Foods

Certain foods may carry risks to people who are considered vulnerable, such as the elderly, the ill, pregnant women, babies, young infants, and those with a compromised immune system.

It is advisable to avoid those foods listed below which belong to a higher-risk category.

There is a slight chance that some eggs carry the bacteria salmonella. To eliminate this risk, cook the eggs until both the yolk and the white are firm. Pay particular attention to dishes and products incorporating lightly cooked or raw eggs, which should be

eliminated from the diet. Sauces including hollandaise and mayonnaise, mousses, soufflés, and meringues all use raw or lightly cooked eggs, as do custard-based dishes, ice creams, and sorbets. These are all considered high-risk foods to the vulnerable groups mentioned above.

Certain meats and poultry also carry the potential risk of salmonella and should be cooked thoroughly until the juices run clear and there is no pinkness left. Unpasteurized products such as milk, cheese (especially soft cheese), pâté, meat (both raw and cooked) all have the potential risk of listeria.

When buying seafood, buy from a reputable source which has a high turnover, to ensure freshness. Fish should have bright, clear eyes, shiny skin, and bright pink or red gills. The fish should feel stiff to the touch, with a slight smell of sea air and iodine. The flesh of fish steaks and fillets should be translucent with no signs of discoloration. Mollusks such as scallops, clams, and mussels are sold fresh, and are still alive. Avoid any that are open or do not close when tapped lightly. In the same way, univalves should withdraw back into their shells when lightly prodded. When choosing cephalopods such as squid and octopus, they should have a firm flesh and pleasant sea smell.

As with all fish, whether it is shellfish or seafish, care is needed when freezing. It is imperative to check whether the fish has been frozen before. If it has been frozen, then it should not be frozen again under any circumstances.

Essential Ingredients

The quantities may differ, but basic baking ingredients do not vary greatly. Let us take a closer look at the baking ingredients that are essential.

Fat

Butter and stick margarine are the fats most commonly used in baking. Others can also be used, such as shortening, lard, and oil. Low-fat spreads are not suitable for baking, as they break down when cooked at a high temperature. Often, it is a matter of personal preference which fat you choose when baking, but there are a few guidelines that are important to remember.

Sweet butter is the fat most commonly used in cake-making, especially in rich fruit cakes and the heavier sponge cakes, such as Madeiras or chocolate tortes. Sweet butter gives a distinctive flavor to the cake. Some people favor margarine, which imparts little or no flavor to the cake. As a rule, firm margarine and butter should not be used straight from the refrigerator, but allowed to come to room temperature before using. Also, fats should first be beaten alone before creaming or mixing. Soft margarine is best suited to one-stage recipes. If oil is used, care should be taken—it is a good idea to follow a specific recipe, as the proportions of oil to flour and eggs are different.

Fat is an integral ingredient when making pastry; again, there are a few specific guidelines to bear in mind.

For short pastry, the best results are achieved by using equal amounts of lard or shortening with butter or stick margarine. The amount of fat used is always half the amount of flour. Other pastries use differing amounts of ingredients. Pâte sucrée (a sweet flan pastry) uses all butter with eggs and a little sugar, while flaky or puff pastry uses a larger proportion of fat to flour and relies on the folding and rolling during mixing to ensure that the pastry rises and flakes well. When using a recipe, refer to the instructions to obtain the best results.

Flour

We can buy a wide range of flours, all designed for specific jobs. Bread flour, which is rich in gluten whether it is white or brown (this includes granary and stone-ground), is best kept for bread and Yorkshire pudding. It is also recommended for steamed suet puddings, as well as puff pastry. Type 00 flour is designed for pasta-making, and there is no substitute for this flour. Ordinary or all-purpose flour is best for cakes, cookies, and sauces, which absorb the fat easily and give a soft, light texture. This flour comes in plain white or self-rising, as well as whole-wheat. Self-rising flour, which has the leavening agent already incorporated, is best kept for sponge cakes, where it is important that an even rising is achieved. All-purpose flour can be used for all types of baking and sauces. If using all-purpose flour for cookies or cakes and puddings, unless otherwise stated in the recipe, use 1 teaspoon of baking powder to 2 cups of flour. With sponge cakes and light fruit cakes, it is best to use self-rising flour, as the leavening agent has already been added to the flour. This way, there is no danger of using too much flour, which can result in a sunken cake with a sour taste. There are other rising agents that are also used. Some cakes use baking soda with or without cream of tartar, blended with warm or sour milk. Beaten eggs also act as a rising agent, since the air trapped in the egg ensures that the mixture rises. Generally no other leavening agent is required.

Also, it is possible to buy flours that contain no gluten. For example, buckwheat, soy, and chickpea flours.

Eggs

When a recipe states 1 egg, it is generally accepted that this refers to a large egg (24 oz per dozen.) Eggs come in a variety of sizes, however, and sometimes when baking, a recipe will state the egg size that should be used. The other egg sizes available, based on their minimum weight per dozen, are: jumbo (30 oz), extra large (27 oz), medium (21 oz), small (18 oz), and peewee (15 oz).

Most hens' eggs on the market have been graded according to quality and size under USDA standards. Eggs are graded AA, A, and B, and the classification is determined by interior and exterior quality.

Interior quality is judged by "candling," an electronic method where the eggs roll over high-intensity lights to allow their insides to be examined. Originally, the eggs were held up to a candle to be inspected, hence the name "candling." The quality of the interior of an egg is determined by the size of the air cell (the space at the large end of the egg between the white and shell), the density and quantity of the white, and whether the yolk is firm and free of defects. In good-quality eggs, the white and the yolk stand higher, and the whites spread less than eggs of a lower quality.

The exterior quality of an egg is determined by a number of factors, such as the soundness, cleanliness, shape, and texture of the eggshell.

The color of the eggshell has nothing to do with either the flavor or the nutritional value of the egg. The shell's color—white or brown—is determined by the type of hen that laid it.

Eggs must always be refrigerated. If eggs are stored at room temperature, they will lose more quality in one day than in a week in the refrigerator. Also, do not remove the eggs from the carton that you bought them in; doing so only exposes them to odor and damage. Store the eggs with the round end uppermost, and in a part of the refrigerator which is separate from foods with strong odors and flavors, such as onions, to make sure the eggs do not absorb any of the strong odors. When baking, and cooking in general, you will achieve the best flavor and quality from the egg if used within a week after purchase. They can, however, be stored for up to one month, providing their shells are not damaged. Allow the eggs to come to room temperature before using.

It is important to remember that raw or semicooked eggs should not be given to babies, toddlers, pregnant women, the elderly, and those suffering from a recurring illness.

Sugar

Sugar not only offers taste to baking, but also adds texture and volume to the mixture. It is generally accepted that superfine sugar is best for sponge cakes, puddings, and meringues. Its fine granules disperse evenly when creaming or whisking. Granulated sugar is used for more general cooking, such as stewing fruit, whereas turbinado sugar, with its toffee taste and crunchy texture, is good for sticky

puddings and pancakes. For rich fruit cakes, Christmas puddings, and cakes, use brown sugar, which gives a rich, intense, molasses flavor.

Confectioners' sugar is used primarily for frostings and can be used in meringues and in fruit sauces when the sugar needs to dissolve quickly.

For a different flavor, try flavoring your own sugar. Place a vanilla bean in a screw-top jar, fill with granulated sugar, screw the lid shut, and leave for 2–3 weeks before using. Top off after use or use thinly pared lemon or orange rind in the same manner.

If trying to reduce sugar intake, then use the unrefined varieties, such as golden granulated, unrefined raw sugar, and the brown sugars. All of these are a little sweeter than their refined counterparts, so less is required. Alternatively, honey or fructose (fruit sugar) can reduce sugar intake, since they have similar calories to sugar, but are twice as sweet. Also, they have a slow release, so their effect lasts longer. Dried fruits can also be included in the diet for this purpose.

Yeast

There is something very comforting about the aroma of freshly baked bread, and the taste is far different and superior to commercially made bread. Bread-making is regarded by some as being a time-consuming process, but with the advent of fast-acting yeast, this no longer applies. There are three types of yeast available: fresh yeast (which freezes well), dried yeast (which is available in cans), and quick-acting yeast, which comes in packets.

Fresh yeast should be bought in small quantities; it has a putty-like color and texture with a slight wine smell. It should be creamed with a little sugar and some warm liquid before being added to the flour.

Dried yeast can be stored for up to six months, and comes in small, hard granules. It should be sprinkled onto warm liquid with a little sugar, then left to stand, normally between 15–20 minutes, until the mixture froths. When replacing the fresh yeast with dried yeast, use 1 tablespoon of dried yeast for 1 oz of fresh yeast.

Quick-acting yeast cuts down the time of bread making and eliminates the need for proofing the bread twice. Also, the yeast can be added straight to the flour without it needing to be activated. When replacing quick-acting yeast for dried yeast, you will need to double the amount.

When using yeast, it is important to remember that it is a fungus and needs food, water, and warmth to work.

Equipment

Nowadays, you can get lost in the cookware sections of some of the larger stores—they really are a cook's paradise with gadgets, cooking tools, and state-of-the-art electronic blenders and mixers. A few, well-chosen, high-quality utensils and pieces of equipment will be frequently used, and will therefore be a much wiser buy than cheaper gadgets.

Cooking equipment not only assists in the kitchen, but can make all the difference between success and failure. Take the humble cake pan: although a very basic piece of cooking equipment, it plays an essential role in baking. Using the correct size is essential. For example, a pan that is too large will spread the mixture too thinly and the result will be a flat, limp-looking cake. On the other hand, cramming the mixture into a pan that is too small will result in the mixture rising up and out of the pan.

Baking Equipment

To ensure successful baking, it is worth investing in a selection of high-quality pans that, if looked after properly, should last for many years. Follow the manufacturers' instructions when first using, and make sure that the pans are thoroughly washed and dried after use and before putting away.

Perhaps the most useful of pans for baking are layer-cake pans, ideal for classics such as sponge cake. You will need two pans, and they are normally 7 or 8 inches in diameter, about 2–3 inches deep, and are often nonstick.

With deep cake pans, it is personal choice whether you buy round or square pans, and they vary in size from 5–14 inches, with a depth between 5–6 inches. A deep cake pan, for everyday fruit or Madeira cake, is a must; a useful size is 8 inches.

Loaf pans are used for bread, fruit, or tea bread and terrines, and normally come in two sizes: 1 lb and 2 lbs.

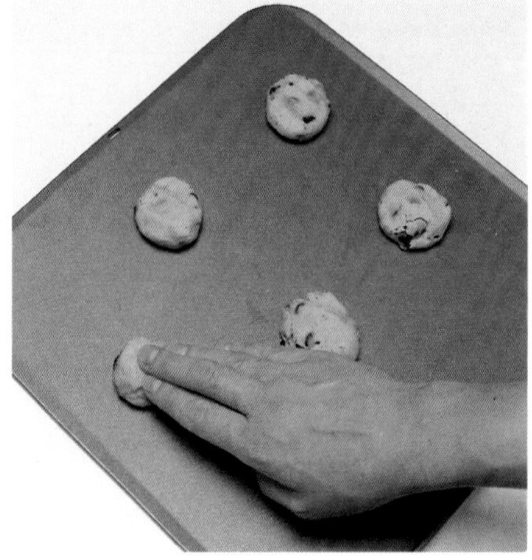

Good cookie sheets are a must for all cooks. Dishes that are too hot to handle, such as apple pies, should be placed directly onto the baking sheet. Meringues, biscuits, and cookies are cooked on the sheet. Do not confuse with jelly-roll pans, which have sides all around, whereas a sheet usually only has one raised side.

Square or oblong shallow baking pans are also very useful for making tray bakes, fudge brownies, bar cookies, and shortbread.

Then there are tartlet tins, ideal for making small buns, jam tarts, or mince pies. One can also find individual custard cups, muffin pans, and tart pans. They are available in a variety of sizes.

There are plenty of other pans to choose from, ranging from themed pans, such as a Christmas tree, numbers, as well as pans shaped as petals, tube pans (pans with a hole in the center), to springform pans, where the sides release after cooking, allowing the finished cake to be easily removed.

Three to four different sizes of mixing bowls are also very useful.

Another piece of equipment which is worth having is a wire cooling rack. It is essential when baking to let cookies and cakes cool after being removed from their pans.

A selection of different-sized roasting pans is also a worthwhile investment, since they can double up as a bain

marie, or for cooking larger quantities of cakes such as gingerbread. A few different pans and dishes are required if baking crisps, soufflés, and pies. Ramekins and small pudding basins can be used for many different recipes, as can small tartlet tins and dariole molds.

When purchasing your implements for baking, the rolling pin is perhaps one of the most important. Ideally, it should be long and thin, heavy enough to roll the pastry out easily, but not too heavy that it is uncomfortable to use. Pastry dough needs to be rolled out on a flat surface, and although a lightly floured flat surface will do, a marble slab will ensure that the dough is kept cool and ensures that the fats do not melt while being rolled. This helps to keep the pastry light, crisp, and flaky, rather than heavy, which happens if the fat melts before being baked.

Other useful basic pastry implements include a pastry brush (which can be used to wet dough or brush on a glaze), a pastry wheel for cutting, and a strainer to remove impurities and also to sift air into the flour, encouraging the pastry or mixture to be lighter in texture.

Basic mixing cutlery, such as a wooden spoon (for mixing and creaming), a spatula (for transferring the mixture from the mixing bowl to the baking pans and spreading the mixture once it is in the pans), and a palette knife (to ease cakes and breads out of their pans before placing them on the wire racks to cool) is also essential. Measuring spoons are necessary for accurate measuring of both dry and wet ingredients.

Electrical Equipment

Nowadays, help from time-saving gadgets and electrical equipment makes baking far easier and quicker. Equipment can be used for creaming, mixing, beating, whisking, kneading, grating, and chopping. There is a wide choice of machines available, from the most basic to the very sophisticated.

Food Processors

First decide what you need your processor to do when choosing a machine. If you are a novice to baking, it may be a waste to start with a machine that offers a wide range of implements and functions. This can be disheartening and result in not using the machine to its full potential.

In general, while styling and product design play a role in the price, the more you pay, the larger the machine will be, with a bigger bowl capacity and many more gadgets attached. Today, you can chop, shred, slice, blend, puree, knead, whisk, and cream anything. However, just what basic features should you make sure your machine has before buying it?

When buying a food processor, look for measurements on the side of the processor bowl and machines with a removable feed tube, which allows food or liquid to be added while the motor is still running. Look for machines that have the ability to increase the capacity of the bowl (ideal when making soup) and have a pulse button for controlled chopping.

For many, storage is an issue, so reversible disks and cord storage, or on more advanced models, a blade storage compartment or box can be advantageous.

It is also worth thinking about machines that offer optional extras, which can be bought as your cooking requirements change. Mini chopping bowls are available for those wanting to chop small quantities of food. If time is an issue, dishwasher-friendly attachments may be important. Citrus presses, liquidizers, and whisks may all be useful attachments for the individual cook.

Blenders

Blenders often come as attachments to food processors, and are generally used for liquidizing and pureeing foods. There are two main types of blenders. The first is known as a goblet blender. The blades of this blender are at the bottom of the goblet, with measurements on the sides. The second blender is portable. It is handheld and should be placed in a bowl to blend.

Food Mixers

These are ideally suited to mixing cakes and kneading dough, either as a tabletop mixer or a handheld mixer. Both are extremely useful and based on the same principle of mixing or beating in an open bowl to allow more air to get to the mixture, and therefore give a lighter texture.

The tabletop mixers are freestanding and are capable of dealing with fairly large quantities of mixture. They are robust machines, capable of dealing easily with kneading dough and heavy cake mixing, as well as whipping cream, beating egg whites, or making one-bowl cakes. These mixers also offer a wide range of attachments, ranging from liquidizers, grinders, juicers, can openers, and many more and varied attachments.

Handheld mixers are smaller than freestanding mixers, and often come with their own bowl and stand from which they can be lifted off and used as handheld devices. They have a motorized head with detachable twin beaters. These mixers are particularly versatile, since they do not need a specific bowl in which to whisk. Any suitable mixing bowl can be used.

Basic Techniques

There is no mystery to successful baking; it really is easy providing you follow a few simple rules and guidelines. First, read the entire recipe before beginning. There is nothing more annoying than getting to the middle of a recipe and discovering that you do not have one or two of the ingredients. Until you are confident, follow a recipe—do not try a shortcut, otherwise you may find that you have left out an important step, which means that the recipe may not work. Most of all, have patience. Baking is easy—if you can read, you can bake.

Pastry Making

Pastry dough needs to be kept as cool as possible throughout. Cool hands help, but are not essential. Use cold or ice water, but not too much, since pastry does not need to be wet. Make sure that your fat is not runny or melted, but firm (this is why solid fat is the best). Avoid using too much flour when rolling out, since this alters the proportions, and also avoid handling the dough too much. Roll in one direction, since this helps to ensure that the dough does not shrink. Let it rest, preferably in the refrigerator, after rolling. If you follow these guidelines, but still the results are not as good as you would like them to be, then make it in a processor instead.

Lining a Tart Pan

It is important to choose the right pan to bake with. You will often find that a loose-bottomed metal tart pan is the best option, since it conducts heat more efficiently and evenly than a ceramic dish. It also has the added advantage of a removable base, which makes the transfer of the final flan or tart a much simpler process; it simply lifts out, keeping the pastry intact.

Roll the pastry dough out on a lightly floured surface, making sure that it is a few inches larger than the pan. Wrap the dough around the rolling pin, lift, and place in the pan. Carefully ease the dough into the base and sides of the pan, ensuring that there are no gaps or tears in the dough. Leave to rest for a few minutes, then trim the edge either with a knife or by rolling a rolling pin across the top of the tart pan.

Baking Blind

The term "baking blind" means that the pastry crust needs to be cooked without the filling, resulting in a crisp pastry shell that is either partially or fully cooked, depending on whether the filling needs any cooking. Pastry shells can be prepared ahead of time as they last for several days if stored correctly in an airtight container, or longer if frozen.

To bake blind, line a pan with the prepared pastry dough and allow to rest in the refrigerator for 30 minutes. This will help to minimize shrinkage while it is being cooked. Remove from the refrigerator and lightly prick the base all over with a fork (do not do this if the filling is runny). Brush with a little beaten egg if desired, or simply line the shell with a large square of waxed paper, big enough to cover both the base and sides of the pastry shell. Fill with either ceramic baking beans or dried beans. Place on a cookie sheet and bake in a preheated oven, generally at 400°F, remembering that ovens can take at least 15 minutes to reach this temperature. Cook for 10–12 minutes, then remove from the oven, and discard the paper and remove the beans. Return to the oven and continue to cook for an additional 5–10 minutes, depending on whether the filling needs cooking. Normally, unless otherwise stated, individual tartlet cases also benefit from baking blind.

Covering a Pie Dish

To cover a pie dish, roll out the pastry dough until it is about two inches larger than the circumference of the dish. Cut a 1-inch strip from around the outside of the dough, and then moisten the edge of the pie dish or pan you are using. Place the strip on the edge of the dish and brush with water

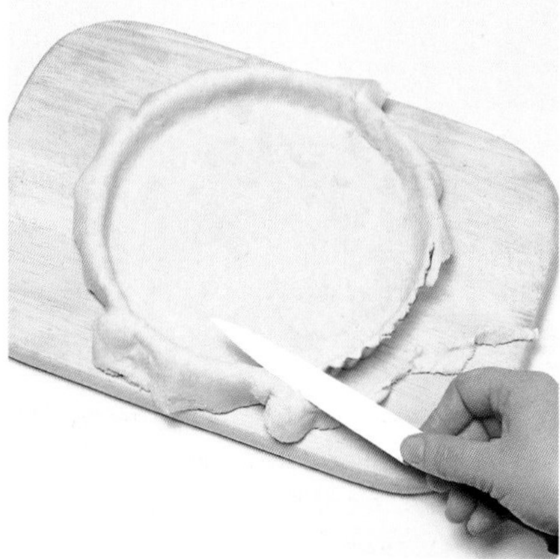

or beaten egg. Generously fill the pie dish until the surface is slightly rounded. Using the rolling pin, lift the remaining dough, and cover the pie dish. Press together, then seal. Using a sharp knife, trim off any excess dough from around the edges. Try to avoid brushing the edges of the dough, especially puff pastry, since this prevents the pastry from rising evenly. Before placing in the oven, make a small hole in the center of the pie to allow the steam to escape.

The edges of the pie can be forked by pressing the back of a fork around the edge of the pie, or instead crimp by pinching the edge crust, holding the thumb and forefinger of your right hand against the edge while gently pushing with the forefinger of your left hand. Other ways of finishing the pie are knocking up (achieved by gently pressing your forefinger down on to the rim and, at the same time, tapping a knife horizontally along the edge, giving it a flaky appearance), or fluting the edges by pressing your thumb down on the edge of the pastry while gently drawing back an all-purpose knife about ½ inch and repeating around the rim. Experiment by putting leaves and berries made out of leftover dough to finish off the pie, then brush the top of the pie with beaten egg.

Lining Cake Pans

If a recipe states that the pan needs lining, do not be tempted to ignore this. Rich fruit cakes and other cakes that take a long time to cook benefit from the pan being lined so that the edges and base do not burn or dry out. Waxed paper or baking parchment is ideal for this. It is a good idea to have the paper at least double thickness, or preferably 3–4 thicknesses. Sponge cakes and other cakes that are cooked in 30 minutes or less are also better if the bases are lined, since it is far easier to remove them from the pan.

The best way to line a round or square pan is to lightly draw around the base and then cut just inside the markings, making it easy to sit in the pan. Next, lightly grease the paper so it easily peels away from the cake. If the sides of the pan also need to be lined, then cut a strip of paper long enough for the pan. This can be measured by wrapping a piece of string around the rim of the pan. Once again, lightly grease the paper, push against the pan, and grease once more, since this will hold the paper to the sides of the pan. Steamed puddings usually need only a disk of waxed paper at the bottom of the dish, as the sides come away easily.

Hints for Successful Baking

Make sure that the ingredients are accurately measured. A cake that has too much flour or insufficient egg will be dry and crumbly. Take care when measuring the leavening agent, if used, since too much will mean that the cake will rise too quickly and then sink. Insufficient rising agent means the cake will not rise in the first place.

Make sure that the oven is preheated to the correct temperature; it can take 10 minutes to reach 350°F. You may find that an oven thermometer is a good investment. Cakes are best if baked in the center of the preheated oven. Do not open the oven door at the beginning of baking, as a draft can make the cake sink. If using a convection oven, then refer to the manufacturers' instructions, as they normally cook 10-20° hotter than conventional ovens.

Check that the cake is thoroughly cooked by removing from the oven and inserting a clean skewer into the cake. Leave for about 30 seconds, then remove. If the skewer is completely clean, then the cake is done: if there is a little mixture left on the skewer, then return the cake to the oven for a few minutes.

Other problems that you may encounter while cake-making are insufficient creaming of the fat and sugar, or a curdled, creamed mixture (which will result in a densely textured and often fairly solid cake). Flour that has not been folded in carefully enough or has not been mixed with enough rising agent may also result in a fairly heavy consistency. It is very important to make sure that the correct size of pan is used, since you may end up either with a flat, hard cake or one that has spilled over the edge of the pan. Another tip to be aware of (especially when cooking with fruit) is that if the consistency is too soft, the cake will not be able to support the fruit.

Finally, when you take your cake out of the oven, unless the recipe states that it should be left in the pan until cold, leave for a few minutes, then loosen the edges and turn out onto a wire rack to cool. Cakes that are left in the pan for too long, unless otherwise stated, tend to sink or slightly overcook.

When storing, make sure the cake is completely cool before placing it into an airtight plastic container.

Culinary Terms Explained

Bain marie A French term, meaning "water bath." Refers to a shallow pan, often a roasting pan, half-filled with water. Smaller dishes of food are then placed in it, allowing them to cook at lower temperatures without overheating. This method is often used to cook custards and other egg dishes, or to keep some dishes warm.

Baking blind The method often used for cooking the pastry shell for flans and tarts before the filling is added. After lining the pan with the uncooked dough, it is then covered with a sheet of waxed paper or baking parchment and weighed down with either ceramic baking beans or dried beans (or sometimes rice), and is baked in the oven as directed.

Baking parchment Used for wrapping food to be cooked (*en papillote*) and for lining cake pans to prevent the cake from sticking to the pan.

Baking powder A leavening agent which works by producing carbon dioxide as a consequence of a reaction caused by the acid and alkali ingredients, which expand during the baking process and make the breads and cakes rise.

Baking soda When combined with liquid, baking soda acts as a rising agent.

Beating The method by which air is introduced into a mixture using a fork, wooden spoon, whisk, or electric mixer. Beating is also used as a method to soften ingredients.

Binding Adding liquid or egg to bring a dry mixture together. Normally, this entails using either a fork, spoon, or your fingertips.

Blender An electric machine with rotating blades used mainly with soft and wet ingredients to puree and liquidize, although it can also grind dry ingredients such as nuts and bread crumbs.

Blending Dry ingredients are mixed with liquid to form a smooth paste, used for thickening stews, casseroles, soups, and sauces.

Brioche A traditional bread eaten in France for breakfast, usually served warm. Brioche has a rich, breadlike texture, contains yeast, and is baked in the shape of a small, round loaf. A delicious substitute for bread in bread and butter pudding.

Caramel Obtained by heating sugar at a very low heat until it turns liquid and deep brown in color. Caramel is used in dishes such as crème caramel, which is, in turn, baked in a bain marie.

Choux A type of pastry (rather like a glossy batter) that is piped into small balls on to a baking sheet and baked until light and airy. They can then be filled with cream or savory fillings.

Cocotte Another name for a ramekin (a small, ovenproof, earthenware pot used for individual portions).

Cornstarch Used to thicken, and can also be used in meringue making to keep the meringue from becoming hard and brittle, and to enhance its texture.

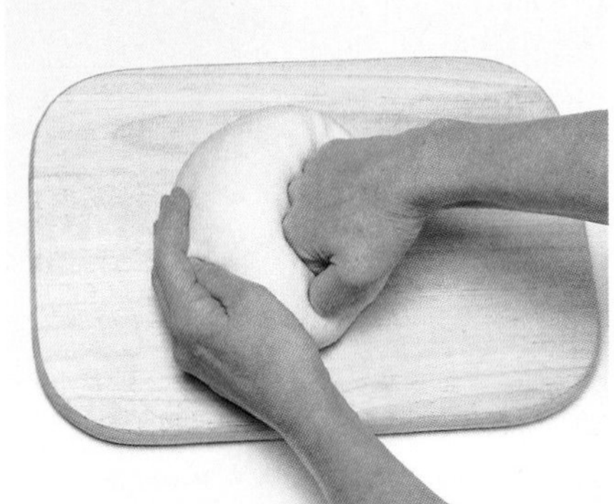

Cream of tartar Another leavening agent often present in both self-rising flour and baking powder.

Creaming The method by which fat and sugar are beaten together until lighter in color and fluffy. By creaming the fat in cake mixtures, air is incorporated into the fairly high fat content. It therefore lightens the texture of cakes and puddings.

Crimping The fluted effect used for the decoration on pies or tarts, created by pinching the edge crust with the thumb and forefinger of your right hand while gently pushing with the forefinger of your left hand.

Crumb The term by which flour and fat are combined, typically for use in pastry, crisps, and cookies.

Curdle When the milk separates from a sauce through acidity or excessive heat. This can also happen to creamed cake mixtures that have separated due to the eggs being too cold or added too quickly.

Dariole A small, narrow mold with sloping sides used for making Madeleines. They can also be used for individual puddings, and molded gelatin desserts.

Dough A dense mixture of flour, water, and, often, yeast. Also used to describe raw pastry, and cookie mixtures.

Dredging The sprinkling of food with a coating (generally of flour or sugar). A board may be dredged with flour before the pastry dough is rolled out, and cakes and cookies can be dredged with sugar or confectioners' sugar after baking.

Dropping Consistency The consistency to which a cake or

pudding mixture reaches before being cooked. It tends to be fairly soft (but not runny), and should drop off a spoon in about five seconds when tapped lightly on the side of a bowl.

Dust To sprinkle lightly, often with flour, sugar, or confectioners' sugar.

En croûte Used to describe food that is covered with raw pastrydough and then baked.

En papillote A French term used to describe food that is baked, but is wrapped in baking parchment before cooking. This works well with fish, since the aroma from the different herbs or spices and the fish are contained during cooking and not released until the paper package is opened.

Fahrenheit (°F) A scale for measuring the temperature of the oven.

Fermenting A term used during bread, beer, or wine making to note the chemical change brought about through the use of a fermenting agent, such as yeast.

Folding A method of combining creamed fat and sugar with flour in cake and pudding mixes, usually by carefully mixing with a large metal spoon, either by cutting and folding, or by doing a figure-eight in order to maintain a light texture.

Glacé A French term meaning "glossy" or "iced." Glacé icing is a quick icing often used to decorate cakes and cookies. It is made using confectioners' sugar and warm water. Candied cherries are sometimes called "glacé cherries."

Grinding Reducing hard ingredients, such as nuts to crumbs, normally by the use of a grinder or a mortar and pestle.

Knead The process of pummeling and working dough in order to strengthen the gluten in the flour and make the dough more elastic, thus allowing it to rise better. In pastry making, the dough is kneaded on a lightly floured surface to give a smooth and elastic dough, making it easier to roll and ensuring an even texture after baking. In both cases, the outside of the dough is drawn into the center.

Pasteurizing The term given when milk and eggs are heated to destroy bacteria.

Phyllo A type of pastry that is wafer-thin. Three to four sheets are usually used at a time in baking.

Piping The way in which cakes and desserts are decorated, or the method by which choux pastry is placed onto a cookie sheet. This is achieved by putting cream, frosting, or mixture in a nylon bag (with a nozzle attached) and then slowly forcing through the nozzle and piping it onto the cake or baking tray.

Proofing The term used in bread making when the bread is allowed to rise a second time after it has been kneaded once and then shaped before it is baked.

Puff pastry Probably the richest of pastries. When making from scratch, it requires the lightest of handling.

Ramekin A small, ovenproof, earthenware dish which provides an individual serving.

Rice paper Edible paper made from the pith of a Chinese tree; it can be used as a base on which to bake sticky cakes and cookies such as almond macaroons.

Rubbing in The method of combining fat into flour for crisp toppings, short-crust pastry, biscuits, and cookies.

Scalloping The term given to a type of pie decoration achieved by horizontal cuts made in the pastry, which is then pulled back with the knife to produce a scalloped effect.

Sifting The shaking of dry ingredients (primarily flour) through a metal or nylon strainer to remove impurities before using in baking. Quantities of flour may also be lightened by using a flour sifter.

Unleavened Often refers to bread which does not use a leavening agent and is therefore flat, such as pita bread.

Vol-au-vent Meaning "to fly on the wind," this small and usually round or oval puff pastry shell is first baked, and then filled with savory meat, seafood, or vegetable filling in a sauce.

Waxed paper Semitransparent paper with a thin coating of wax on each side. Because it is moisture-proof and nonstick, it is extremely useful when baking for lining cake pans. Traditionally, it was used to cover foods, but today most people tend to use plastic wrap or aluminum foil. Not advisable for use in the oven if exposed, as it may smoke or burn.

Whipping/whisking The term given to incorporating air rapidly into a mixture (either through using a manual whisk or an electric mixer).

Zest Very thin, long pieces of the colored part of an orange, lemon, or lime peel, containing the fruit oil that is responsible for the citrus flavor. Normally, a zester is used to remove the zest without any of the bitter white pith. (Rind refers to the peel which has been grated on a grater into very small pieces.)

Everyday Cakes

The following section enables you to prepare a range of popular cakes by simply following the step-by-step instructions and clear picture guides. From the classic Baked Lemon & Raisin Cheesecake to the refreshingly contemporary Cappuccino Cakes, there are recipes to tempt every taste.

Apple & Cinnamon Crisp-top Cake

INGREDIENTS

Cuts into 8 slices

For the topping:

¾ lb eating apples, peeled
1 tbsp lemon juice
1 cup/¼ lb self-rising flour
1 tsp ground cinnamon
¾ stick/3 oz butter or margarine
⅓ cup/3 oz light brown sugar
1 tbsp milk

For the base:

1 stick plus 1 tbsp/4½ oz butter or margarine
⅔ cup/4½ oz superfine sugar
2 eggs
1¼ cups/5 oz self-rising flour
Cream or freshly made custard sauce, to serve

1 Preheat the oven to 350°F, 10 minutes before baking. Lightly grease and line the bottom of an 8-inch, deep, round cake pan with waxed paper.

2 Finely chop the apples and mix with the lemon juice. Set aside while making the cake.

3 For the crisp topping, sift the flour and cinnamon together into a large bowl.

4 Rub the butter or margarine into the flour and cinnamon until the mixture resembles coarse bread crumbs.

5 Stir the sugar into the bread crumbs and set aside.

6 For the base, cream the butter or margarine and sugar together until light and fluffy. Gradually beat the eggs into the sugar and butter mixture a little at a time until all the egg has been added.

7 Sift the flour and gently fold in with a metal spoon or rubber spatula.

8 Spoon into the bottom of the prepared cake pan. Arrange the apple pieces on top, then lightly stir the milk into the crisp mixture.

9 Scatter the crisp mixture over the apples and bake in the preheated oven for 1½ hours. Serve cold with cream or custard sauce.

TASTY TIP

For a crunchier-textured topping, stir in ½ cup/2 oz of chopped, mixed nuts and seeds to the crisp mixture in step 5.

2

6

9

Chocolate & Coconut Cake

INGREDIENTS

Cuts into 8 slices

- $\frac{1}{4}$ lb semisweet chocolate, roughly chopped
- $\frac{3}{4}$ cup/6 oz butter or margarine
- $\frac{3}{4}$ cup/6 oz superfine sugar
- 3 eggs, beaten
- $1\frac{1}{2}$ cups/6 oz self-rising flour
- 1 tbsp unsweetened cocoa
- $\frac{3}{4}$ cup/2 oz shredded coconut

For the frosting:

- $\frac{1}{2}$ cup/$\frac{1}{4}$ lb butter or margarine
- 2 tbsp creamed coconut
- 2 cups/$\frac{1}{2}$ lb confectioners' sugar
- $\frac{1}{3}$ cup/1 oz shredded coconut, lightly toasted

TASTY TIP

Why not experiment with the chocolate in this recipe? For a different taste, try using orange-flavored bittersweet chocolate or add 1–2 tablespoons of rum when melting the chocolate.

1 Preheat the oven to 350°F, 10 minutes before baking. Melt the chocolate in a small bowl placed over a saucepan of gently simmering water, making sure that the bottom of the bowl does not touch the water. When the chocolate has melted, stir until smooth and let cool.

2 Lightly grease and line the bottoms of 2 7-inch, round cake pans with waxed paper or baking parchment. In a large bowl beat the butter or margarine and sugar together with a wooden spoon until light and creamy. Beat in the eggs a little at a time, then stir in the melted chocolate.

3 Sift the flour and unsweetened cocoa together and gently fold into the chocolate mixture with a metal spoon or rubber spatula. Add the shredded coconut and mix lightly. Divide between the 2 prepared pans and smooth the tops.

4 Bake in the preheated oven for 25–30 minutes, or until a skewer comes out clean when inserted into the center of the cake. Let cool in the pan for 5 minutes, then turn out, discard the lining paper and leave on a wire rack until cold.

5 Beat together the butter or margarine and creamed coconut until light. Add the confectioners' sugar and mix well. Spread half of the frosting on 1 layer and press the cakes together. Spread the remaining frosting over the top, sprinkle with the shredded coconut, and serve.

1

4

5

Victoria Sponge with Mango & Mascarpone

INGREDIENTS

Cuts into 8 slices

3/4 cup/6 oz superfine sugar, plus extra for dusting
1 1/2 cups/6 oz self-rising flour, plus extra for dusting
1 1/2 sticks/6 oz butter or margarine
3 extra-large eggs
1 tsp vanilla extract
1/4 cup/1 oz confectioners' sugar
1 1/8 cups/9 oz mascarpone cheese
1 large ripe mango, peeled

1 Preheat the oven to 375°F, 10 minutes before baking. Lightly grease 2 7-inch cake pans and lightly dust with superfine sugar and flour, tapping the pans to remove any excess.

2 In a large bowl cream the butter or margarine and sugar together with a wooden spoon until light and creamy.

3 In another bowl mix the eggs and vanilla extract together. Sift the flour several times onto a plate.

4 Beat a little egg into the butter and sugar, then a little flour and beat well.

5 Continue adding the flour and eggs alternately, beating between each addition, until the mixture is well mixed and smooth. Divide the mixture between the 2 prepared cake pans, level the surface, then using the back of a large spoon, make a slight dip in the center of each cake.

6 Bake in the preheated oven for 25–30 minutes, until the center of the cake springs back when gently pressed with a clean finger. Turn out onto a wire rack and leave the cakes until cold.

7 Beat the confectioners' sugar and mascarpone cheese together, then chop the mango into small cubes.

8 Use half the mascarpone and mango to sandwich the cakes together. Spread the rest of the mascarpone on top, decorate with the remaining mango and serve. Otherwise lightly cover and store in the refrigerator. Use within 3–4 days.

TASTY TIP

Mango has been used in this recipe, but 1/2 cup/1/4 lb of mashed strawberries could be used instead. Reserve a few whole strawberries, slice and use to decorate the cake.

1

5

6

Almond Cake

INGREDIENTS

Cuts into 8 slices

1 cup/½ lb butter or margarine
1 cup/½ lb superfine sugar
3 extra-large eggs
1 tsp vanilla extract
1 tsp almond extract
1 cup/¼ lb self-rising flour
1½ cups/6 oz ground almonds
⅓ cup/2 oz whole almonds, blanched
1 square/1 oz semisweet chocolate

1 Preheat the oven to 300°F. Lightly grease and line the bottom of an 8-inch, deep, round cake pan with waxed paper or baking parchment.

2 Cream together the butter or margarine and sugar with a wooden spoon until light and fluffy.

3 Beat the eggs and extracts together. Gradually add to the sugar and butter mixture, and mix well between each addition.

4 Sift the flour, and mix with the ground almonds. Beat into the egg mixture until mixed well and smooth. Pour into the prepared cake pan.

5 Roughly chop the whole almonds and sprinkle over the cake before baking in the preheated oven.

6 Bake in the preheated oven for 45 minutes, or until golden and risen, and a skewer inserted into the center of the cake comes out clean.

7 Remove from the pan and leave to cool on a wire rack. Melt the chocolate in a small bowl placed over a saucepan of gently simmering water, stirring until smooth and free of lumps.

8 Drizzle the melted chocolate over the cooled cake and serve once the chocolate has set.

TASTY TIP

Baking with ground almonds helps to keep the cake moist as well as adding a slightly nutty flavor to the cake. 1–2 tablespoons of orange water can be added with the zest of 1 orange in step 4 if a fragrant citrus flavor is desired, but do omit the vanilla extract.

2

5

8

Lemon Drizzle Cake

INGREDIENTS

Cuts into 16 squares

1 stick plus 1 tbsp/1/4 lb butter or margarine
3/4 cup/6 oz superfine sugar
2 extra-large eggs
1 1/2 cups/6 oz self-rising flour
2 lemons, preferably unwaxed
1/4 cup/2 oz superfine sugar

1 Preheat the oven to 350°F, 10 minutes before baking. Lightly grease and line the bottom of a 7-inch, square cake pan with baking parchment.

2 In a large bowl, cream the butter or margarine and superfine sugar together until soft and fluffy.

3 Beat the eggs, then gradually add a little of the egg to the creamed mixture, adding 1 tablespoon of flour after each addition.

4 Finely grate the rind from 1 of the lemons and stir into the creamed mixture, beating well until smooth. Squeeze the juice from the lemon, strain, then stir into the mixture.

5 Spoon into the prepared pan, level the surface and bake in the preheated oven for 25–30 minutes. Using a zester remove the peel from the last lemon and mix with 1/8 cup/1 oz of the superfine sugar and set aside.

6 Squeeze the juice into a small saucepan. Add the rest of the superfine sugar to the lemon juice in the saucepan and heat gently, stirring occasionally.

7 When the sugar has dissolved, simmer gently for 3–4 minutes until syrupy.

8 Prick the cake all over with a fine skewer, to let the syrup to soak in.

9 Sprinkle the lemon zest and sugar over the top of the cake, drizzle over the syrup and leave to cool in the pan. Cut the cake into squares and serve.

FOOD FACT

This classic cake is a favorite in many kitchens. The buttery sponge is perfectly complemented by the lemon syrup, which soaks into the cake giving it a gooeyness which is even better the next day!

3

5

9

Jelly Roll

INGREDIENTS

Cuts into 8 slices

- $^{3}/_{4}$ cup/3 oz self-rising flour
- 3 eggs
- 1 tsp vanilla extract
- 7 tbsp superfine sugar
- $^{1}/_{4}$ cup/1 oz hazelnuts, toasted and finely chopped
- 3 tbsp apricot preserve
- $1^{1}/_{4}$ cups/$^{1}/_{2}$ pint heavy cream, lightly whipped

1 Preheat the oven to 425°F, 15 minutes before baking. Lightly grease and line the bottom of a 9 x 13-inch jelly-roll pan with a single sheet of nonstick baking parchment.

2 Sift the flour several times, then set on top of the oven to warm a little.

3 Place a mixing bowl with the eggs, vanilla extract, and sugar over a pan of hot water, making sure that it is not touching the water.

4 With the saucepan off the heat, beat with an electric hand mixer until the egg mixture becomes pale and mousse-like and has increased in volume.

5 Remove the bowl from the saucepan and continue to beat for an additional 2–3 minutes. Sift in the flour and very gently fold in using a metal spoon or rubber spatula, taking care not to knock out the air beaten in already. Pour into the prepared pan tilting to make sure that the mixture is evenly distributed. Bake in the preheated oven for 10–12 minutes, or until well risen, golden brown, and the top springs back when lightly touched.

6 Sprinkle the toasted, chopped hazelnuts over a large sheet of waxed paper.

7 When the cake has cooked turn out onto the hazelnut covered paper, and trim the edges of the cake. Holding an edge of the paper with the short side of the cake nearest you, roll up the cake.

8 When fully cold, carefully unroll and spread with the apricot preserve and then the cream. Roll back up and serve. Otherwise, store in the refrigerator and eat within 2 days.

TASTY TIP

Any flavor of preserve can be used in this recipe. While apricot preserve is delicious, traditional raspberry or blackcurrant preserve also works very well. In place of the cream why not try butter cream frosting or beaten mascarpone as a filling?

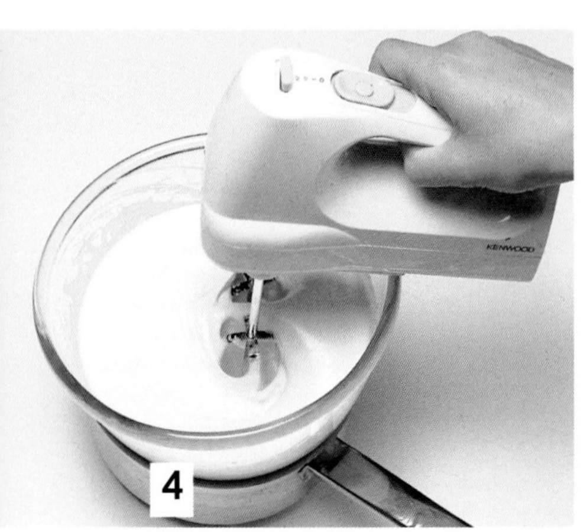

4

7

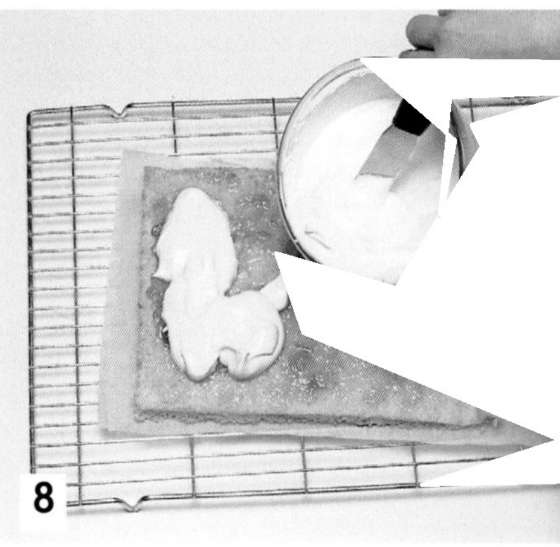
8

Toffee Apple Cake

INGREDIENTS

Cuts into 8 slices

- 2 small eating apples, peeled
- 4 tbsp soft dark brown sugar
- 1½ sticks/6 oz butter or margarine
- ¾ cup/6 oz superfine sugar
- 3 eggs
- 1½ cups/6 oz self-rising flour
- ⅔ cup/¼ pint heavy cream
- 2 tbsp confectioners' sugar
- ½ tsp vanilla extract
- ½ tsp ground cinnamon

1. Preheat the oven to 350°F, 10 minutes before baking time. Lightly grease and line the bottoms of 2 8-inch cake pans with waxed paper or baking paper.
2. Thinly slice the apples and toss in the brown sugar until well coated. Arrange them over the bottom of the prepared pans and set aside.
3. Cream together the butter or margarine and superfine sugar until light and fluffy.
4. Beat the eggs together in a small bowl and gradually beat them into the creamed mixture, beating well between each addition.
5. Sift the flour into the mixture, and using a metal spoon or rubber spatula, fold in.
6. Divide the mixture between the 2 cake pans and level the surface.
7. Bake in the preheated oven for 25–30 minutes, until golden and well risen. Leave in the pans to cool.
8. Lightly whip the cream with 1 tablespoon of the confectioners' sugar and the vanilla extract.
9. Sandwich the cakes together with the cream. Mix the remaining confectioners' sugar and ground cinnamon together, sprinkle over the top of the cake and serve.

TASTY TIP

The dark brown sugar used in this recipe could be replaced with a golden brown sugar to give a deliciously rich toffee flavor to the apples. When baked, the sugar will melt slightly into a caramel consistency.

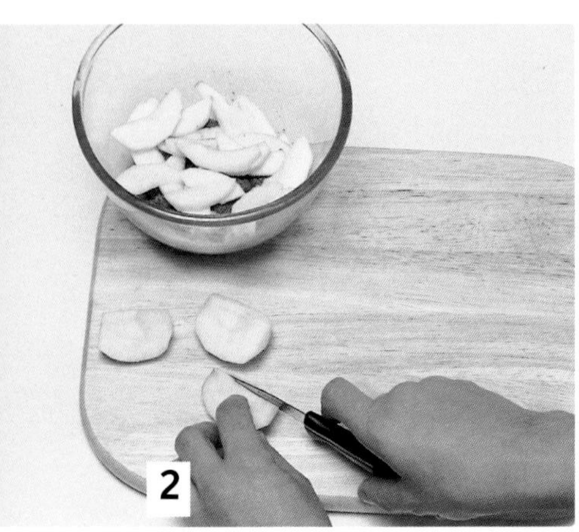
2

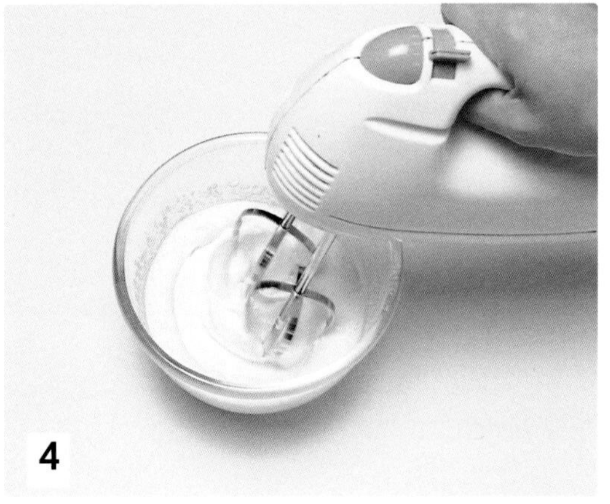
4

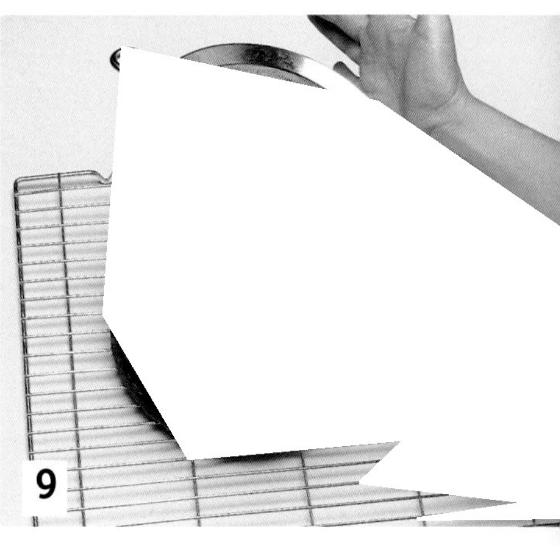
9

Cappuccino Cakes

INGREDIENTS

Makes 6

$\frac{1}{2}$ cup/$\frac{1}{4}$ lb butter or margarine
$\frac{1}{2}$ cup/$\frac{1}{4}$ lb superfine sugar
2 eggs
1 tbsp strong black coffee
1$\frac{1}{4}$ cups/5 oz self-rising flour
$\frac{1}{2}$ cup/$\frac{1}{4}$ lb mascarpone cheese
1 tbsp confectioners' sugar, sifted
1 tsp vanilla extract
unsweetened cocoa, sifted, to dust

1. Preheat the oven to 375°F, 10 minutes before baking. Place 6 large paper baking cups into a muffin pan or alternatively place on a cookie sheet.
2. Cream the butter or margarine and sugar together until light and fluffy. Break the eggs into a small bowl and beat lightly with a fork.
3. Using a wooden spoon, beat the eggs into the butter and sugar mixture a little at a time, until they are all incorporated.
4. If the mixture looks curdled, beat in a spoonful of the flour to return the mixture to a smooth consistency. Finally, beat in the black coffee.
5. Sift the flour into the mixture, then with a metal spoon or rubber spatula, gently fold in the flour.
6. Place spoonfuls of the mixture into the baking cups.
7. Bake in the preheated oven for 20–25 minutes, or until risen and springy to the touch. Cool on a wire rack.
8. In a small bowl, beat together the mascarpone cheese, confectioners' sugar, and vanilla extract.
9. When the cakes are cool, spoon the vanilla mascarpone on top of each one. Dust with unsweetened cocoa and serve. Store in the refrigerator and eat within 24 hours.

TASTY TIP

The combination of coffee with the vanilla-flavored mascarpone is heavenly! Make sure, however, that you use a good-quality coffee in this recipe. Colombian coffee is generally good and at its best possesses a smooth rounded flavor.

4

6

9

Fruit Cake

INGREDIENTS

Cuts into 10 slices

2 sticks/$\frac{1}{2}$ lb butter or margarine
1 scant cup/7 oz soft brown sugar
rind of 1 orange, finely grated
1 tbsp black molasses
3 extra-large eggs, beaten
2$\frac{1}{2}$ cups/10 oz all-purpose flour
$\frac{1}{4}$ tsp ground cinnamon
$\frac{1}{2}$ tsp pumpkin spice
pinch freshly grated nutmeg
$\frac{1}{4}$ tsp baking soda
$\frac{1}{2}$ cup/3 oz candied peel
$\frac{1}{4}$ cup/2 oz candied cherries
$\frac{2}{3}$ cup/$\frac{1}{4}$ lb raisins
$\frac{2}{3}$ cup/$\frac{1}{4}$ lb golden raisins
$\frac{2}{3}$ cup/$\frac{1}{4}$ lb ready-to-eat dried apricots, chopped

TASTY TIP

For a fruit cake with a kick, remove the cake from the oven when cooked and leave to cool. When the cake has cooled, turn out and make holes in the bottom of the cake with a skewer. Dribble over 4–5 tablespoons of your favorite alcohol such as whisky, brandy, or Drambuie.

1. Preheat the oven to 300°F, 10 minutes before baking. Lightly grease and line a 9-inch, deep, round cake pan with a double thickness of waxed paper.
2. In a large bowl, cream together the butter or margarine, sugar, and orange rind, until light and fluffy, then beat in the molasses.
3. Beat in the eggs a little at a time, beating well between each addition.
4. Set aside 1 tablespoon of the flour. Sift the remaining flour, the spices, and baking soda into the mixture.
5. Mix all the fruits and the rest of the flour together, then stir into the cake mixture.
6. Turn into the prepared pan and smooth the top, making a small hollow in the center of the cake mixture.
7. Bake in the preheated oven for 1 hour, then reduce the heat to 275°F.
8. Bake for a further 1$\frac{1}{2}$ hours, or until cooked and a skewer inserted into the center comes out clean. Leave to cool in the pan, then turn the cake out and serve. Otherwise, when cold store in an airtight pan.

2

5

6

Banana Cake

INGREDIENTS

Cuts into 8 slices

3 ripe bananas
1 tsp lemon juice
3/4 cup/5 oz soft brown sugar
3/4 stick/3 oz butter or margarine
2 1/4 cups/9 oz self-rising flour
1 tsp ground cinnamon
3 eggs
1/2 cup/2 oz walnuts, chopped
1 tsp each ground cinnamon and superfine sugar, to decorate
fresh cream, to serve

HELPFUL HINT

The riper the bananas used in this recipe the better! Look out for reductions in supermarkets and fruit shops as ripe bananas are often sold very cheaply. This cake tastes really delicious the day after it has been made—the sponge solidifies slightly yet does not lose any moisture. Eat within 3–4 days.

1 Preheat the oven to 375°F, 10 minutes before baking. Lightly grease and line the bottom of a 7-inch, deep, round cake pan with waxed paper or baking parchment.

2 Mash 2 of the bananas in a small bowl, sprinkle with the lemon juice and a heaped tablespoon of the sugar. Mix together lightly and set aside.

3 Gently heat the remaining sugar and butter or margarine in a small saucepan until the butter has just melted.

4 Pour into a small bowl, then let cool slightly. Sift the flour and cinnamon into a large bowl and make a well in the center.

5 Beat the eggs into the cooled sugar mixture, pour into the well of flour, and mix thoroughly.

6 Gently stir in the mashed banana mixture. Pour half of the mixture into the prepared pan. Thinly slice the remaining banana and arrange over the cake mixture.

7 Sprinkle over the chopped walnuts, then cover with the remaining cake mixture.

8 Bake in the preheated oven for 50–55 minutes, or until well risen and golden brown. Let cool in the pan, turn out and sprinkle with the ground cinnamon and superfine sugar. Serve hot or cold with a pitcher of fresh cream for pouring.

2

5

7

Coffee & Pecan Cake

INGREDIENTS

Cuts into 8 slices

$1\frac{1}{3}$ cups/6 oz self-rising flour
$\frac{1}{2}$ cup/$\frac{1}{4}$ lb butter or margarine
$\frac{3}{4}$ cup/6 oz brown sugar
1 tbsp instant coffee
2 extra-large eggs
$\frac{1}{2}$ cup/2 oz pecans, roughly chopped

For the frosting:

1 tsp instant coffee
1 tsp unsweetened cocoa
6 tbsp/3 oz unsalted butter, softened
$1\frac{1}{2}$ cups/6 oz confectioners' sugar, sifted
whole pecans, to decorate

HELPFUL HINT

To enjoy this cake whenever you want, simply bake in bulk. Follow the recipe up to step 5, then when the cakes have cooled wrap in waxed paper or kitchen foil and freeze. When desired, remove from the freezer and let defrost at room temperature. Serve with or without frosting.

1 Preheat the oven to 375°F, 10 minutes before baking. Lightly grease and line the bottoms of 2 7-inch sandwich pans with waxed paper or baking parchment. Sift the flour and set aside.

2 Beat the butter or margarine and sugar together until light and creamy. Dissolve the coffee in 2 tablespoons of hot water and let cool.

3 Lightly mix the eggs with the coffee liquid. Gradually beat into the creamed butter and sugar, adding a little of the sifted flour with each addition.

4 Fold in the pecans, then divide the mixture between the prepared pans and bake in the preheated oven for 20–25 minutes, or until well risen and firm to the touch.

5 Leave to cool in the pans for 5 minutes before turning out and cooling on a wire rack.

6 To make the frosting, blend together the coffee and unsweetened cocoa with enough boiling water to make a stiff paste. Beat into the butter and confectioners' sugar.

7 Sandwich the 2 cakes together using half of the frosting. Spread the remaining frosting over the top of the cake and decorate with the whole pecans to serve. Store in an airtight container.

3

4

6

Carrot Cake

INGREDIENTS

Cuts into 8 slices

1¾ cups/7 oz all-purpose flour
½ tsp ground cinnamon
½ tsp nutmeg, freshly grated
1 tsp baking powder
1 tsp baking soda
¾ cup/5 oz golden brown sugar
1 scant cup/7 fl oz vegetable oil
3 eggs
½ lb carrots, peeled and roughly grated
½ cup/2 oz walnuts, chopped

For the frosting:

¾ cup/6 oz cream cheese
rind of 1 orange, finely grated
1 tbsp orange juice
1 tsp vanilla extract
1 cup/¼ lb confectioners' sugar

TASTY TIP

For a fruitier cake, add 1 grated apple and ⅓ cup/2 oz of dried golden raisins in step 5. To plump up the dried golden raisins, soak for an hour, or overnight in 1¼ cups/½ pint of cold tea.

1 Preheat the oven to 300°F, 10 minutes before baking. Lightly grease and line the bottom of a 6-inch, deep, square cake pan with waxed paper or baking parchment.

2 Sift the flour, spices, baking powder, and baking soda together into a large bowl.

3 Stir in the golden brown sugar and mix together.

4 Lightly beat the oil and eggs together, then gradually stir into the flour and sugar mixture. Stir well.

5 Add the carrots and walnuts. Mix thoroughly, then pour into the prepared cake pan. Bake in the preheated oven for 1¼ hours, or until light and springy to the touch, and a skewer inserted into the center of the cake comes out clean.

6 Remove from the oven and let cool in the pan for 5 minutes before turning out onto a wire rack. Set aside until cold.

7 To make the frosting, beat together the cream cheese, orange rind, orange juice, and vanilla extract. Sift the confectioners' sugar and stir into the cream cheese mixture.

8 When cold, discard the lining paper, spread the cream cheese frosting over the top, and serve cut into squares.

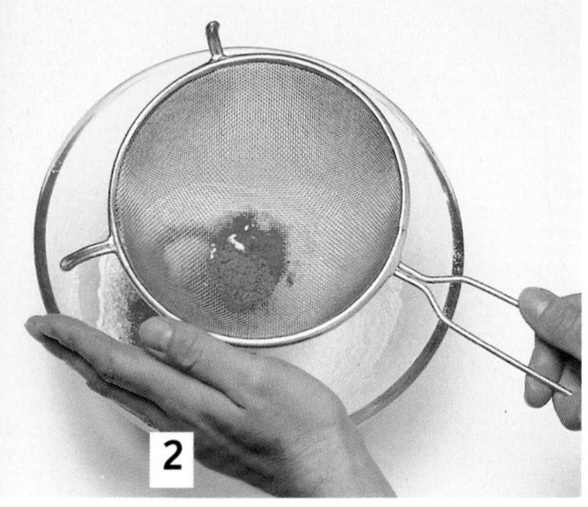

Whisked Sponge Cake

INGREDIENTS

Cuts into 6 slices

1 cup/$^1/_4$ lb all-purpose flour, plus 1 tsp
$^3/_4$ cup/6 oz superfine sugar, plus 1 tsp
3 eggs
1 tsp vanilla extract
4 tbsp raspberry jelly
$^1/_2$ cup/2 oz fresh raspberries, crushed
confectioners' sugar, to dust

1 Preheat the oven to 400°F, 15 minutes before baking. Mix 1 teaspoon of the flour and 1 teaspoon of the sugar together. Lightly grease 2
7-inch layer-cake pans and dust lightly with the sugar and flour.

2 Place the eggs in a large heatproof bowl. Add the sugar, then place over a saucepan of gently simmering water, making sure that the bottom of the bowl does not touch the hot water. Using an electric mixer, beat the sugar and eggs until they become light and fluffy. (The whisk should leave a trail in the mixture when it is lifted out.)

3 Remove the bowl from the saucepan of water, add the vanilla extract, and continue beating for 2–3 minutes. Sift the flour gently into the egg mixture and, using a metal spoon or rubber spatula, carefully fold in, taking care not to overmix and remove all the air that has been beaten in.

4 Divide the mixture between the 2 prepared cake pans. Tap lightly on the work surface to remove any air bubbles. Bake in the preheated oven for 20–25 minutes, or until golden. Test that the cake is ready by gently pressing the center with a clean finger—it should spring back.

5 Leave to cool in the pans for 5 minutes, then turn out onto a wire rack. Blend the jelly and the crushed raspberries together. When the cakes are cold, spread over the jelly mixture and sandwich the cakes together. Dust the top with confectioners' sugar and serve.

TASTY TIP

For a creamier low-fat filling, mix the crushed raspberries or strawberries with 4 tablespoons each of plain yogurt and low-fat sour cream.

1

2

5

Marble Cake

INGREDIENTS

Cuts into 8 slices

2 sticks/½ lb butter or margarine
1 cup/½ lb superfine sugar
4 eggs
2 cups/½ lb self-rising flour, sifted
finely grated rind and juice of 1 orange
¼ cup/1 oz unsweetened cocoa, sifted

For the topping:

zest and juice of 1 orange
1 tbsp superfine sugar

HELPFUL HINT

This cake has a wonderful combination of rich chocolate and orangey sponge. It is important not to swirl too much in step 2, as the desired effect is to have blocks of different colored sponge.

1. Preheat the oven to 375°F, 10 minutes before baking. Lightly grease and line the bottom of an 8-inch, deep, round cake pan with waxed paper or baking parchment.
2. In a large bowl, cream the butter or margarine and sugar together until light and fluffy.
3. Beat the eggs together. Beat into the creamed mixture a little at a time, beating well between each addition. When all the egg has been added, fold in the flour with a metal spoon or rubber spatula.
4. Divide the mixture equally between 2 bowls. Beat the grated orange rind into one of the bowls with a little of the orange juice. Mix the unsweetened cocoa with the remaining orange juice until smooth, then add to the other bowl and beat well.
5. Spoon the mixture into the prepared pan, in alternate spoonfuls. When all the cake mixture is in the pan, take a skewer and swirl it in the 2 mixtures.
6. Tap the bottom of the pan on the work surface to level the mixture. Bake in the preheated oven for 50 minutes, or until cooked, and a skewer inserted into the center of the cake comes out clean.
7. Remove from the oven and leave in the pan for a few minutes before cooling on a wire rack. Discard the lining paper.
8. For the topping, place the orange zest and juice with the superfine sugar in a small saucepan and heat gently until the sugar has dissolved. Bring to a boil and simmer gently for 3–4 minutes, until the juice is syrupy. Pour over the cooled cake and serve when cool. Otherwise, store in an airtight container.

4

5

8

Rich Chocolate Cup Cakes

INGREDIENTS

Makes 12

1½ cups/6 oz self-rising flour
¼ cup/1 oz unsweetened cocoa
¾ cup/6 oz light brown sugar
¾ stick/3 oz butter, melted
2 eggs, lightly beaten
1 tsp vanilla extract
2 tbsp/1½ oz maraschino cherries, drained and chopped

For the chocolate frosting:

2 squares/2 oz unsweetened chocolate
¼ cup/1 oz unsalted butter
¼ cup/1 oz confectioners' sugar, sifted

For the cherry frosting:

1 cup/¼ lb frosting sugar
2 tbsp/¼ oz unsalted butter, melted
1 tsp syrup from the maraschino cherries
3 maraschino cherries, halved, to decorate

1 Preheat the oven to 350°F, 10 minutes before baking. Line a 12-hole muffin or deep bun pan with baking cups. Sift the flour and unsweetened cocoa into a bowl. Stir in the sugar, then add the melted butter, eggs, and vanilla extract. Beat together with a wooden spoon for 3 minutes or until well blended.

2 Divide half the mixture between 6 of the baking cups. Dry the cherries thoroughly on paper towels, then fold into the remaining mixture and spoon into the rest of the baking cups. (The cakes should only come about three-quarters of the way up the baking cups and have flat tops to allow the frosting to be spooned over.)

3 Bake on the shelf above the center of the preheated oven for 20 minutes, or until a skewer inserted into the center of a cake comes out clean. Transfer to a wire rack and leave to cool.

4 For the chocolate frosting, melt the chocolate and butter in a heatproof bowl set over a saucepan of hot water. Remove from the heat and leave to cool for 3 minutes, stirring occasionally. Stir in the confectioners' sugar. Spoon over the 6 plain chocolate cakes and leave to set.

5 For the cherry frosting, sift the confectioners' sugar into a bowl and stir in 1 tablespoon of boiling water, the butter, and cherry syrup. Spoon the frosting over the remaining 6 cakes, decorate each with a halved cherry, and leave to set.

1

3

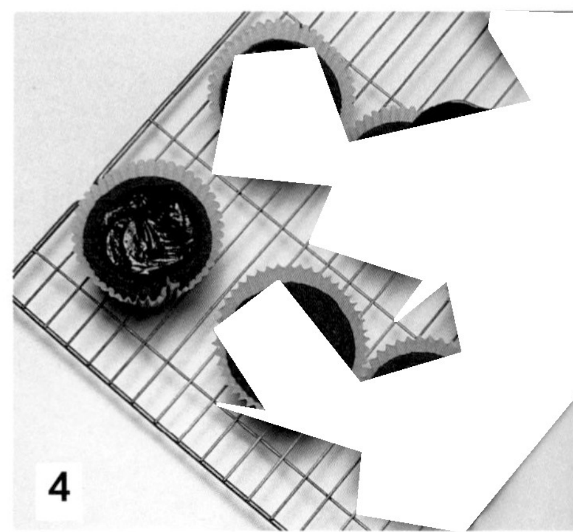
4

All-in-one Chocolate Fudge Cakes

INGREDIENTS

Makes 15 squares

- 3/4 cup/6 oz firmly packed dark brown sugar
- 1 1/2 sticks/6 oz butter, softened
- 1 1/4 cups/5 oz self-rising flour
- 1/2 tsp/1 oz unsweetened cocoa
- 1/2 tsp baking powder
- pinch salt
- 3 eggs, lightly beaten
- 1 tbsp corn syrup

For the fudge topping:

- 3/4 cup/3 oz superfine sugar
- 2/3 cup/1/4 pint evaporated milk
- 6 squares/6 oz unsweetened chocolate, coarsely chopped
- 3 tbsp/1 1/2 oz unsalted butter, softened
- 1 cup/1/4 lb soft fudge candies, finely chopped

1 Preheat the oven to 350°F, 10 minutes before baking. Grease and line an 11 x 7 x 1-inch cake pan with nonstick baking parchment.

2 Place the soft brown sugar and butter in a bowl, and sift in the flour, unsweetened cocoa, baking powder, and salt. Add the eggs and corn syrup, beat with an electric mixer for 2 minutes, then add 2 tablespoons of warm water and beating for an additional minute.

3 Turn the mixture into the prepared pan and level the top with the back of a spoon. Bake on the center shelf of the preheated oven for 30 minutes, or until firm to the touch. Turn the cake out onto a wire rack and leave to cool before removing the baking parchment.

4 To make the topping, gently heat the sugar and evaporated milk in a saucepan, stirring frequently until the sugar has dissolved. Bring the mixture to a boil and simmer for 6 minutes, without stirring.

5 Remove the mixture from the heat. Add the chocolate and butter, and stir until melted and blended. Pour into a bowl and chill in the refrigerator for 1–2 hours or until thickened. Spread the topping over the cake, then sprinkle with the chopped fudge. Cut the cake into 15 squares before serving.

TASTY TIP

Use a mixture of fudge candies for the topping on this cake, including chocolate, vanilla, and toffee flavors.

2

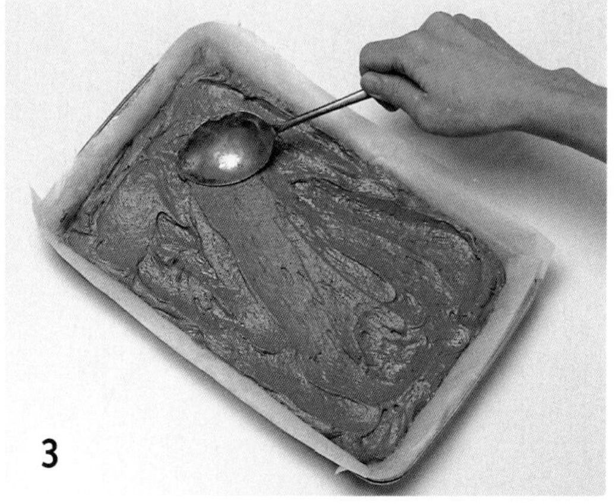
3

5

Orange Chocolate Cheesecake

INGREDIENTS

Serves 8

$1\frac{1}{2}$ cups/$\frac{1}{2}$ lb Graham crackers
$\frac{1}{2}$ stick/2 oz butter
4 cups/1 lb mixed fruits, such as blueberries and raspberries
1 tbsp confectioners' sugar, sifted
few sprigs fresh mint, to decorate

For the filling:

2 cups/1 lb soft cream cheese
1 tbsp powdered gelatin
12 squares/$\frac{3}{4}$ lb orange chocolate, broken into segments
$2\frac{1}{2}$ cups/1 pint heavy cream

1 Lightly grease and line an 8-inch, round, loose-based cake pan with nonstick baking parchment. Place the Graham crackers in a plastic bag and crush using a rolling pin. Alternatively, use a food processor. Melt the butter in a medium-sized heavy-based saucepan, add the crushed Graham crackers, and mix well. Press the mixture into the bottom of the lined pan, then chill in the refrigerator for 20 minutes.

2 For the filling, remove the cream cheese from the refrigerator at least 20 minutes before using, to allow the cheese to come to room temperature. Place the cream cheese in a bowl, and beat until smooth. Set aside.

3 Pour 4 tablespoons of water into a small bowl and sprinkle over the gelatin. Leave to stand for 5 minutes until spongy. Place the bowl over a saucepan of simmering water and let dissolve, stirring occasionally. Leave to cool slightly.

4 Melt the orange chocolate in a heatproof bowl set over a saucepan of simmering water, then leave to cool slightly.

5 Whip the cream until soft peaks form. Beat the gelatin and chocolate into cream cheese. Fold in the cream. Spoon into the pan and level the surface. Chill in the refrigerator for 4 hours until set.

6 Remove the cheesecake from the pan and place on a serving plate. Top with the fruits, dust with confectioners' sugar, and decorate with sprigs of mint.

HELPFUL HINT

Always add gelatin to the mixture you are working with and beat well to evenly distribute it. Never add the mixture to the gelatin or it will tend to set in a lump.

1

5

6

Baked Lemon & Golden Raisin Cheesecake

INGREDIENTS

Cuts into 10 slices

1 1/3 cups/10 oz superfine sugar
1/2 stick/2 oz butter
1/2 cup/2 oz self-rising flour
1/2 level tsp baking powder
5 extra-large eggs
2 cups/1 lb cream cheese
1/3 cup/1 1/2 oz all-purpose flour
grated rind of 1 lemon
3 tbsp fresh lemon juice
1/2 cup/1/4 pint sour cream
1/2 cup/3 oz golden raisins

To decorate:

1 tbsp confectioners' sugar
fresh blackcurrants or blueberries
mint leaves

TASTY TIP

Vary the flavor by adding a little freshly grated nutmeg and 1/2 teaspoon of ground cinnamon to the base in step 2. Add a little of both spices to the confectioners' sugar before sprinkling.

1 Preheat the oven to 325°F. Grease an 8-inch, loose-bottomed, round cake pan with nonstick baking parchment.

2 Beat 1/4 cup/2 oz of the sugar and the butter together until light and creamy, then stir in the self-rising flour, baking powder, and 1 egg.

3 Mix lightly together until well blended. Spoon into the prepared pan and spread the mixture over the bottom. Separate the 4 remaining eggs and set aside.

4 Blend the cheese in a food processor until soft. Gradually add the egg yolks and sugar, and blend until smooth. Turn into a bowl and stir in the rest of the flour, lemon rind, and juice.

5 Mix lightly before adding the sour cream and golden raisins, stirring well.

6 Beat the egg whites until stiff, fold into the cheese mixture, and pour into the pan. Tap lightly on the surface to remove any air bubbles. Bake in the preheated oven for about 1 hour, or until golden and firm.

7 Cover lightly if browning too much. Switch the oven off and leave in the oven to cool for 2–3 hours.

8 Remove the cheesecake from the oven and when completely cold remove from the pan. Sprinkle with the confectioners' sugar, decorate with the blackcurrants or blueberries and mint leaves, and serve.

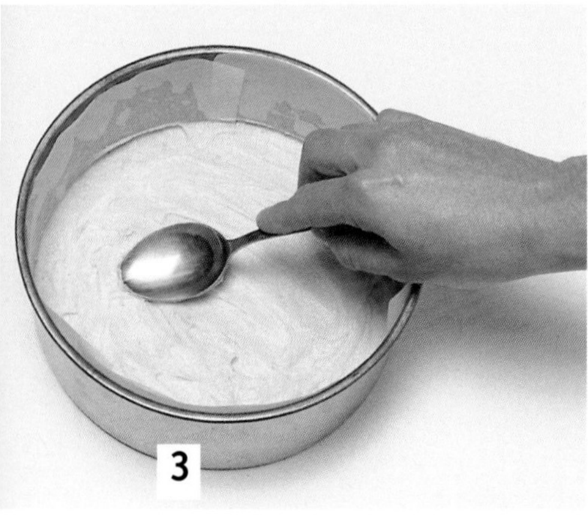

Cakes for Special Occasions

Whether you are planning to amaze your guests or simply wish to indulge yourself, these easy-to-prepare recipes will never fail to impress. This varied selection of delicious cakes ranges from the richly chocolate to the lightly fruity.

Apricot & Almond Layer Cake

INGREDIENTS

Cuts into 8–10 slices

1¼ sticks/5 oz unsalted butter, softened
½ cup/¼ lb superfine sugar
5 eggs, separated
5 squares/5 oz unsweetened chocolate, melted and cooled
1¼ cups/5 oz self-rising flour, sifted
½ cup/2 oz ground almonds
¾ cup/3 oz confectioners' sugar, sifted
¾ cup/11 oz apricot jelly
1 tbsp amaretto liqueur
1 stick/¼ lb unsalted butter, melted
4 squares/¼ lb unsweetened chocolate, melted

1 Preheat the oven to 350°F, 10 minutes before baking. Lightly grease and line 2 9-inch, round cake pans. Cream the butter and sugar together until light and fluffy, then beat in the egg yolks, one at a time, beating well after each addition. Stir in the cooled chocolate with 1 tablespoon cooled boiled water, then fold in the flour and ground almonds.

2 Beat the egg whites until stiff, then gradually beat in the confectioners' sugar, beating well after each addition. Beat until the mixture is stiff and glossy, then fold it into the chocolate mixture in 2 batches.

3 Divide the mixture evenly between the prepared pans and bake in the preheated oven for 30–40 minutes or until firm. Leave for 5 minutes before turning out onto wire racks. Leave to cool completely.

4 Split the cakes in half. Gently heat the jelly, pass through a strainer, and stir in the amaretto liqueur. Place 1 cake layer onto a serving plate. Spread with a little of the jelly, then sandwich with the next layer. Repeat with all the layers and use any remaining jelly to brush over the entire cake. Leave until the jelly sets.

5 Meanwhile, beat the butter and chocolate together until smooth, then cool at room temperature until thick enough to spread. Cover the top and sides of the cake with the chocolate frosting and leave to set before slicing and serving.

HELPFUL HINT

Use a very good-quality apricot jelly as it is a major flavor in the finished cake.

1

2

4

Mocha Truffle Cake

INGREDIENTS

Cuts into 8–10 slices

3 eggs
½ cup/¼ lb superfine sugar
⅓ cup/1½ oz cornstarch
⅓ cup/1½ oz self-rising flour
2 tbsp unsweetened cocoa
2 tbsp milk
2 tbsp coffee liqueur
3½ squares/3½ oz white chocolate, melted and cooled
7 squares/7 oz unsweetened chocolate, melted and cooled
2 cups/1 pint heavy cream
7 squares/7 oz semisweet chocolate
¾ stick/3½ oz unsalted butter

1 Preheat the oven to 350°F, 10 minutes before baking. Lightly grease and line a 9-inch, deep, round cake pan. Beat the eggs and sugar in a bowl until thick and creamy.

2 Sift together the cornstarch, self-rising flour, and unsweetened cocoa, and fold lightly into the egg mixture. Spoon into the prepared pan and bake in the preheated oven for 30 minutes or until firm. Turn out onto a wire rack and leave until cold. Split the cold cake horizontally into 2 layers. Mix together the milk and coffee liqueur, and brush onto the cake layers.

3 Put the cooled white chocolate into one bowl and the cooled unsweetened chocolate into another one. Whip the cream until soft peaks form, then divide between the 2 bowls and stir. Place 1 layer of cake in a 9-inch springform pan. Spread with half the white chocolate cream. Top with the unsweetened chocolate cream, then the remaining white chocolate cream, finally place the remaining cake layer on top. Chill in the refrigerator for 4 hours or overnight until set.

4 When ready to serve, melt the semisweet chocolate and butter in a heatproof bowl set over a saucepan of simmering water, and stir until smooth. Remove from the heat and leave until thick enough to spread, then use to cover the top and sides of the cake. Let set at room temperature, then chill in the refrigerator. Cut the cake into slices and serve.

HELPFUL HINT

Unless you are going to make a lot of chocolate or coffee desserts, liqueurs are very expensive to buy. Look for superstore own-label brands or miniatures.

1

2

3

Chocolate Buttermilk Cake

INGREDIENTS

Cuts into 8–10 slices

1½ sticks/6 oz butter
1 tsp vanilla extract
1½ cups/¾ lb superfine sugar
4 eggs, separated
¾ cup/3½ oz self-rising flour
¼ cup/1½ oz unsweetened cocoa
¼ cup/6 fl oz buttermilk
7 squares/7 oz unsweetened chocolate
¾ stick/3½ oz butter
1 cup/½ pint heavy cream

1 Preheat the oven to 350°F, 10 minutes before baking. Lightly grease and line a 9-inch, deep, round cake pan. Cream together the butter, vanilla extract, and sugar until light and fluffy, then beat in the egg yolks, 1 at a time.

2 Sift together the flour and cocoa and fold into the egg mixture together with the buttermilk. Beat the egg whites until soft peaks form and fold carefully into the chocolate mixture in 2 batches. Spoon the mixture into the prepared pan and bake in the preheated oven for 1 hour or until firm. Cool slightly, then turn out onto a wire rack and leave until completely cold.

3 Place the chocolate and butter together in a heatproof bowl set over a saucepan of simmering water and heat until melted. Stir until smooth, then leave at room temperature until the chocolate is thick enough to spread.

4 Split the cake horizontally in half. Use some of the chocolate mixture to sandwich the 2 halves together. Spread and decorate the top of the cake with the remaining chocolate mixture. Finally, whip the cream until soft peaks form and use to spread around the sides of the cake. Chill in the refrigerator until required. Serve cut into slices. Store in the refrigerator.

TASTY TIP

If buttermilk is unavailable, measure ¾ cup/6 fl oz of whole milk and add 2 teaspoons of lemon juice or white wine vinegar. Leave to stand for 1 hour at room temperature and then use as above.

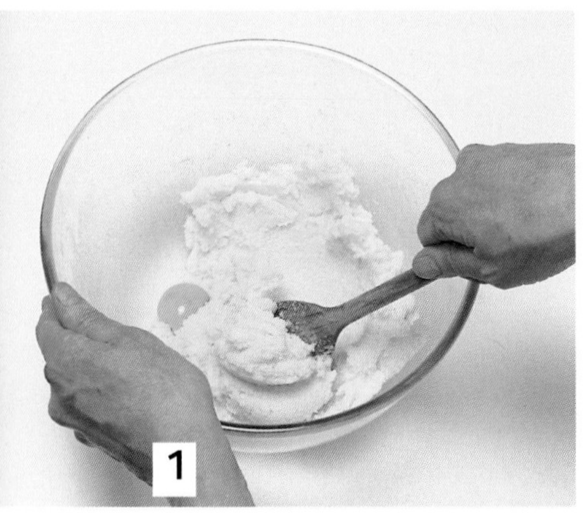
1

2

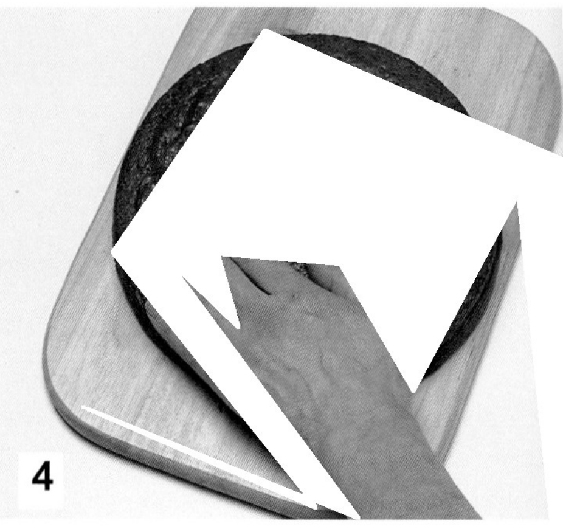
4

Peach & White Chocolate Cake

INGREDIENTS

Cuts into 8–10 slices

1½ sticks/6 oz unsalted butter, softened
2 tsp grated orange rind
¾ cup/6 oz superfine sugar
3 eggs
3½ squares/3½ oz white chocolate, melted and cooled
2 cups/½ lb self-rising flour, sifted
1 cup/½ pint heavy cream
4⅓ cups/1½ oz confectioners' sugar
1 cup/¼ lb hazelnuts, toasted and chopped

For the peach filling:

2 ripe peaches, peeled and chopped
2 tbsp peach or orange liqueur
1 cup/½ pint heavy cream
⅓ cup/1½ oz confectioners' sugar

1 Preheat the oven to 325°F, 10 minutes before baking. Lightly grease and line a 9-inch, deep, round cake pan. Cream the butter, orange rind, and sugar together until light and fluffy. Add the eggs, 1 at a time, beating well after each addition, then beat in the cooled white chocolate.

2 Add the flour and ¾ cup/6 fl oz of water in 2 batches. Spoon into the prepared pan and bake in the preheated oven for 1½ hours or until firm. Leave to stand for at least 5 minutes before turning out onto a wire rack to cool completely.

3 To make the filling, place the peaches in a bowl and pour over the liqueur. Let stand for 30 minutes. Whip the cream with the confectioners' sugar until soft peaks form, then fold in the peach mixture.

4 Split the cold cake in to 3 layers, place 1 layer on a serving plate, and spread with half the peach filling. Top with a second sponge layer and spread with the remaining peach filling. Top with the remaining cake.

5 Whip the cream and confectioners' sugar together until soft peaks form. Spread over the top and sides of the cake, piping some onto the top if liked. Press the hazelnuts into the side of cake and if liked sprinkle a few on top. Chill in the refrigerator until required. Serve cut into slices. Store the cake in the refrigerator.

TASTY TIP

When fresh peaches are out of season, use drained and chopped canned peaches instead.

1

2

3

Dark Chocolate Layered Torte

INGREDIENTS

Cuts into 10–12 slices

1½ sticks/6 oz butter
1 tbsp instant coffee grounds
5 squares/ 5 oz unsweetened chocolate
1½ cups/¾ lb superfine sugar
1¼ cups/5 oz self-rising flour
1 cup/¼ lb all-purpose flour
2 tbsp unsweetened cocoa
2 eggs
1 tsp vanilla extract
7½ squares/7½ oz unsweetened chocolate, melted
1 stick/¼ lb butter, melted
⅓ cup/1½ oz confectioners' sugar, sifted
2 tsp raspberry jelly
2½ tbsp chocolate liqueur
¾ cup/3½ oz slivered almonds, toasted

1 Preheat the oven to 300°F, 10 minutes before baking. Lightly grease and line a 9 inch square cake pan. Melt the butter in a saucepan, remove from the heat, and stir in the coffee grounds and 1 cup/8 fl oz hot water. Add the unsweetened chocolate and sugar, and stir until smooth, then pour into a bowl.

2 In another bowl, sift together the flours and unsweetened cocoa. Using an electric mixer, beat the sifted mixture into the chocolate mixture until smooth. Beat in the eggs and vanilla extract. Pour into the pan and bake in the preheated oven for 1¼ hours or until firm. Leave for at least 5 minutes before turning out onto a wire rack to cool.

3 Meanwhile, mix together 7 squares of the melted unsweetened chocolate with the butter and confectioners' sugar and beat until smooth. Leave to cool, then beat again. Set aside 4–5 tablespoons of the chocolate filling.

4 Cut the cooled cake in half to make 2 rectangles, then split each rectangle in 3 horizontally. Place 1 cake layer on a serving plate and spread thinly with the jelly, then a thin layer of chocolate filling. Top with a second cake layer and sprinkle with a little liqueur, then spread thinly with filling. Repeat with the remaining cake layers, liqueur, and filling.

5 Chill in the refrigerator for 2–3 hours or until firm. Cover the cake with the remaining chocolate filling and press the slivered almonds into the sides of the cake.

6 Place the remaining melted chocolate in a nonstick baking parchment decorating bag. Snip a small hole in the tip and pipe thin lines crossways over the cake. Drag a skewer lengthways through the frosting in alternating directions to create a feathered effect. Serve.

TASTY TIP

Use unsweetened chocolate that has 70 per cent cocoa solids in this cake for the best flavor.

3

4

6

Chocolate Mousse Sponge

INGREDIENTS

Cuts into 8–10 slices

3 eggs
1/3 cup/3 oz superfine sugar
1 tsp vanilla extract
1/2 cup/2 oz self-rising flour, sifted
1/4 cup/1 oz ground almonds
2 squares/2 oz unsweetened chocolate, grated
confectioners' sugar, for dusting
freshly sliced strawberries, to decorate

For the mousse:

2 sheets gelatin
1/4 cup/2 fl oz heavy cream
3 1/2 squares/3 1/2 oz unsweetened chocolate, chopped
1 tsp vanilla extract
4 egg whites
1/2 cup/1/4 lb superfine sugar

TASTY TIP

Sheet gelatin is very easy to use. Soak the gelatin as described in step 2, then squeeze out the excess liquid. It must be added to hot liquid, where it will melt on contact.

1 Preheat the oven to 350°F, 10 minutes before baking. Lightly grease and line a 9-inch, round cake pan, and lightly grease the sides of a 9-inch springform pan. Beat the eggs, sugar, and vanilla extract until thick and creamy. Fold in the flour, ground almonds, and unsweetened chocolate. Spoon the mixture into the prepared round cake pan and bake in the preheated oven for 25 minutes or until firm. Turn out onto a wire rack to cool.

2 For the mousse, soak the gelatin in 1/4 cup/2 fl oz of cold water for 5 minutes until softened. Meanwhile, heat the heavy cream in a small saucepan, when almost boiling, remove from the heat and stir in the chocolate and vanilla extract. Stir until the chocolate melts. Squeeze the excess water out of the gelatin and add to the chocolate mixture. Stir until dissolved, then pour into a large bowl.

3 Beat the egg whites until stiff, then gradually add the superfine sugar, beating well between each addition. Fold the egg-white mixture into the chocolate mixture in 2 batches.

4 Split the cake into 2 layers. Place 1 layer in the bottom of the springform pan. Pour in the chocolate mousse mixture, then top with the second layer of cake. Chill in the refrigerator for 4 hours or until the mousse has set. Loosen the sides and remove the cake from the pan. Dust with confectioners' sugar and decorate the top with a few freshly sliced strawberries. Serve cut into slices.

1

3

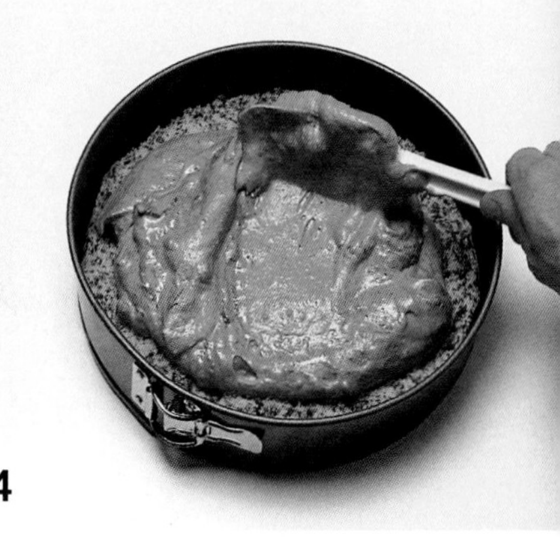
4

Chocolate Chiffon Cake

INGREDIENTS

Cuts into 10–12 slices

1/2 cup/2 oz unsweetened cocoa
2 3/4 cups/11 oz self-rising flour
2 1/2 cups/1 1/4 lb superfine sugar
7 eggs, separated
1/4 cup/4 fl oz vegetable oil
1 tsp vanilla extract
3/4 cup/3 oz walnuts
7 squares/7 oz unsweetened chocolate, melted

For the frosting:

1 1/2 sticks/6 oz butter
2 1/2 cups/10 oz confectioners' sugar, sifted
2 tbsp unsweetened cocoa, sifted
2 tbsp brandy

HELPFUL HINT

Do not overmix the mixture in step 2 or the cake will be heavy instead of very light and spongy.

1 Preheat the oven to 325°F, 10 minutes before baking. Lightly grease and line a 9-inch, round cake pan. Lightly grease a cookie sheet. Blend the unsweetened cocoa with 3/4 cup/6 fl oz boiling water and let cool. Place the flour and 1 1/2 cups/3/4 lb of the superfine sugar in a large bowl, and add the cocoa mixture, egg yolks, oil, and vanilla extract. Beat until smooth and lighter in color.

2 Beat the egg whites in a clean, grease-free bowl until soft peaks form, then fold into the cocoa mixture.

3 Pour into the prepared pan and bake in the preheated oven for 1 hour or until firm. Leave for 5 minutes before turning out onto a wire rack to cool.

4 To make the frosting, cream together 1 stick/1/4 lb of the butter with the confectioners' sugar, cocoa, and brandy until smooth, then set aside. Melt the remaining butter and blend with 5 squares/5 oz of the melted chocolate. Stir until smooth and then leave until thickened.

5 Place the remaining superfine sugar into a heavy saucepan over a low heat and heat until it has melted and is a deep golden brown.

6 Add the walnuts and the remaining melted chocolate to the melted sugar and pour onto the prepared baking sheet. Leave until cold and brittle, then chop finely. Set aside.

7 Split the cake into 3 layers, place 1 layer onto a serving plate and spread with half of the brandy butter frosting. Top with a second cake layer, spread with the remaining brandy butter frosting, and arrange the third cake layer on top. Cover the cake with the thickened chocolate glaze. Sprinkle with the walnut praline and serve.

2

6

7

Sachertorte

INGREDIENTS

Cuts into 10–12 slices

5 squares/5 oz unsweetened chocolate
1¼ sticks/5 oz unsalted butter, softened
½ cup/¼ lb superfine sugar, plus 2 tbsp
3 eggs, separated
1¼ cups/5 oz all-purpose flour, sifted

To decorate:

⅔ cup/½ lb apricot jelly
4 squares/¼ lb unsweetened chocolate, chopped
1 stick/¼ lb unsalted butter
1 square/1 oz semisweet chocolate

FOOD FACT

In 1832, the Viennese foreign minister asked a Vienna hotel to prepare an especially tempting cake. The head pastry chef was ill and so the task fell to second year apprentice, Franz Sacher, who presented this delightful cake.

1 Preheat the oven to 350°F, 10 minutes before baking. Lightly grease and line a 9-inch, deep cake pan.

2 Melt the chocolate in a heatproof bowl set over a saucepan of simmering water. Stir in 1 tablespoon of water and let cool.

3 Beat the butter and ½ cup/¼ lb of the sugar together until light and fluffy. Beat in the egg yolks, one at a time, beating well between each addition. Stir in the melted chocolate, then the flour.

4 In a clean grease-free bowl, beat the egg whites until stiff peaks form, then beat in the remaining sugar. Fold into the chocolate mixture and spoon into the prepared pan. Bake in the preheated oven for 30 minutes until firm. Leave for 5 minutes, then turn out onto a wire rack to cool. Leave the cake upside down.

5 To decorate the cake, split the cold cake in 2 and place one half on a serving plate. Heat the jelly and rub through a fine strainer.

6 Brush half the jelly onto the first cake half, then cover with the remaining cake layer, and brush with the remaining jelly. Leave at room temperature for 1 hour or until the jelly has set.

7 Place the unsweetened chocolate with the butter into a heatproof bowl set over a saucepan of simmering water, and heat until the chocolate has melted. Stir occasionally until smooth, then leave until thickened. Use to cover the cake.

8 Melt the semisweet chocolate in a heatproof bowl set over a saucepan of simmering water. Place in a small wax decorating bag and snip a small hole at the tip. Pipe "Sacher" with a large "S" on the top. Let set at room temperature.

3

4

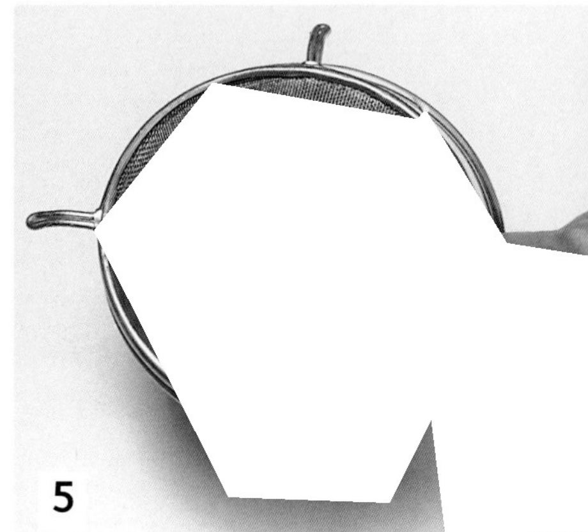
5

Sacher

Chocolate Roulade

INGREDIENTS

Cuts into 8 slices

7 squares/7 oz unsweetened chocolate
1 cup/7 oz superfine sugar
7 eggs, separated
1 cup/½ pint heavy cream
3 tbsp Cointreau or orange-flavored liqueur
4 tbsp confectioners' sugar, for dusting

To decorate:

fresh raspberries
sprigs fresh mint

TASTY TIP

Leaving the cake in the pan overnight gives it a fudgy texture and also means that the cake is less likely to break when it is rolled up.

1 Preheat the oven to 350°F, 10 minutes before baking. Lightly grease and line a 13 x 9-inch jelly-roll pan with nonstick baking parchment.

2 Break the chocolate into small pieces into a heatproof bowl set over a saucepan of simmering water. Leave until almost melted, stirring occasionally. Remove from the heat and leave to stand for 5 minutes.

3 Beat the egg yolks with the sugar until pale and creamy and the whisk leaves a trail in the mixture when lifted, then carefully fold in the melted chocolate.

4 In a clean grease-free bowl, beat the egg whites until stiff, then fold 1 large spoonful into the chocolate mixture.

5 Mix lightly, then gently fold in the remaining egg whites. Pour the mixture into the prepared pan and level the surface. Bake in the preheated oven for 20–25 minutes or until firm.

6 Remove the cake from the oven, leave in the pan, and cover with a wire rack and a damp dish towel. Leave for 8 hours or overnight.

7 Dust a large sheet of nonstick baking parchment generously with 2 tablespoons of the confectioners' sugar. Unwrap the cake and turn out onto the new paper. Remove the old baking parchment.

8 Whip the cream with the liqueur until soft peaks form. Spread over the cake, leaving a 1 inch border all around.

9 Using the paper to help, roll the cake up from a short end. Transfer to a serving plate, seam-side down, and dust with the remaining confectioners' sugar. Decorate with fresh raspberries and mint. Serve.

1

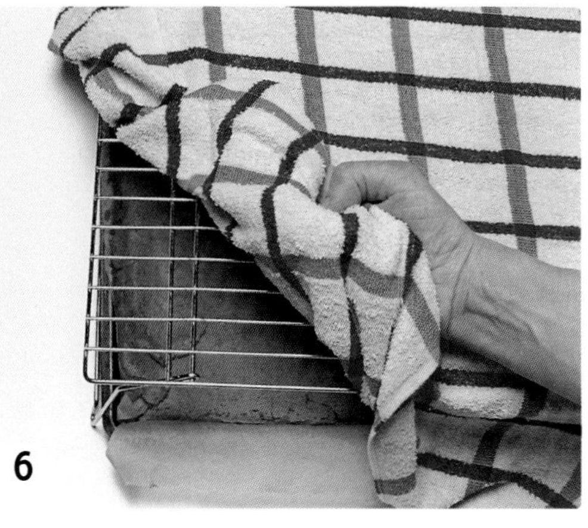
6

9

Supreme Chocolate Cake

INGREDIENTS

Cuts into 10–12 slices

For the cake:

1½ cups/6 oz self-rising flour, sifted
1½ tsp baking powder, sifted
3 tbsp unsweetened cocoa, sifted
1½ sticks/6 oz margarine or butter, softened
¾ cup/6 oz superfine sugar
3 eggs

To decorate:

12 squares/¾ lb unsweetened chocolate
1 gelatin leaf
1 cup/7 fl oz heavy cream
¾ stick/3 oz butter
unsweetened cocoa, for dusting

1 Preheat the oven to 350°F, 10 minutes before baking. Lightly grease and line 2 8-inch, round cake pans. Place all the cake ingredients into a bowl and beat together until thick, add a little warm water if very thick. Divide the mixture evenly between the prepared pans. Bake in the preheated oven for 35–40 minutes until a skewer inserted in the center comes out clean. Cool on wire racks.

2 Very gently heat 2 tablespoons hot water with 2 squares/2 oz of the chocolate and stir until combined. Remove from the heat and leave for 5 minutes. Place the gelatin in a shallow dish and add 2 tablespoons cold water. Leave for 5 minutes, then squeeze out any excess water and add to the chocolate and water mixture. Stir until dissolved. Whip the heavy cream until just thickened. Add the chocolate mixture and continue beating until soft peaks form. Leave until starting to set.

3 Place 1 of the cakes onto a serving plate and spread with half the cream mixture. Top with a second cake and the remaining cream, cover with the third cake, and chill in the refrigerator until the cream has set.

4 Melt 6 squares/6 oz of the chocolate with the butter, and stir until smooth. Let thicken. Melt the remaining chocolate. Cut 12 4-inch squares of kitchen foil. Spread the chocolate evenly over the squares to within 1 inch of the edges. Refrigerate for 3–4 minutes until just set, but not brittle. Gather up the corners and crimp together. Return to the refrigerator until firm.

5 Spread the chocolate and butter mixture over the top and sides of the cake. Remove the foil from the giant curls and use to decorate the top of the cake. Dust with unsweetened cocoa and serve cut into wedges.

HELPFUL HINT

If you prefer, make ordinary chocolate curls to decorate this cake.

1

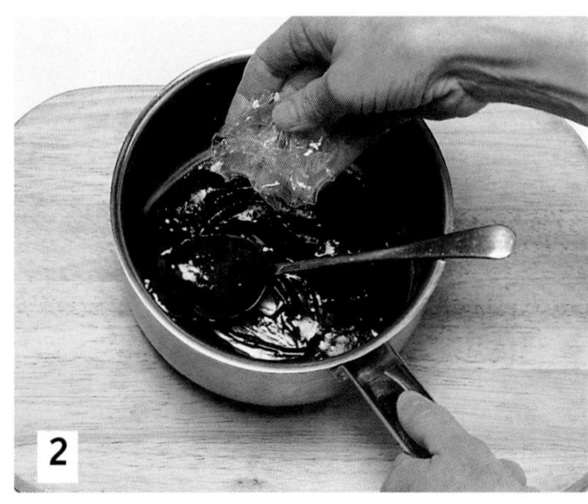
2

4

Black Forest Cake

INGREDIENTS

Cuts 10–12 slices

2$^1/_4$ sticks/9 oz butter
1 tbsp instant coffee grounds
1$^1/_2$ cups/12 fl oz hot water
7 squares/7 oz unsweetened chocolate, chopped or broken
1$^3/_4$ cups/14 oz superfine sugar
2 cups/$^1/_2$ lb self-rising flour
1$^1/_4$ cups/5 oz all-purpose flour
$^1/_2$ cup/2 oz unsweetened cocoa
2 eggs
2 tsp vanilla extract
2 x 14-oz cans pitted cherries in juice
2 tsp arrowroot
2 cups/1 pint heavy cream
$^1/_4$ cup/2 fl oz kirsch

1 Preheat the oven to 300°F, 5 minutes before baking. Lightly grease and line a 9-inch, deep cake pan.

2 Melt the butter in a large saucepan. Blend the coffee with the hot water, add to the butter with the chocolate and sugar, and heat gently, stirring until smooth. Pour into a large bowl and leave until just warm.

3 Sift together the flours and unsweetened cocoa. Using an electric mixer, beat the warm chocolate mixture on a low speed, then gradually beat in the dry ingredients. Beat in the eggs 1 at a time, then the vanilla extract.

4 Pour the mixture into the prepared pan and bake in the preheated oven for 1$^3/_4$ hours or until firm and a skewer inserted into the center comes out clean. Leave in the pan for 5 minutes to cool slightly before turning out onto a wire rack.

5 Place the cherries and their juice in a small saucepan and heat gently. Blend the arrowroot with 2 teaspoons water until smooth, then stir into the cherries. Cook, stirring, until the liquid thickens. Simmer very gently for 2 minutes, then leave until cold.

6 Beat the heavy cream until thick. Trim the top of the cake if necessary, then split the cake into 3 layers.

7 Brush the bottom of the cake with half the kirsch. Top with a layer of cream and one-third of the cherries. Repeat the layering, then place the third layer on top. Set aside a little cream for decorating and use the remainder to cover the top and sides of the cake. Pipe a decorative edge around the cake, then arrange the remaining cherries in the center, and serve.

HELPFUL HINT

The cake can be assembled and served straightaway but will benefit from being refrigerated for 1–2 hours so that the cream sets slightly. This will make slicing easier.

3

5

6

Whole Orange & Chocolate Cake with Marmalade Cream

INGREDIENTS

Cuts into 6–8 slices

1 small orange, scrubbed
2 eggs, separated, plus 1 whole egg
1¼ cups/5 oz superfine sugar
1 cup/¼ lb ground almonds
3 squares/3 oz unsweetened chocolate, melted
½ cup/3½ fl oz heavy cream
¾ cup/7 oz cream cheese
¼ cup/1 oz confectioners' sugar
2 tbsp orange marmalade
orange zest, to decorate

TASTY TIP

This cake contains no flour and is therefore likely to sink in the center on cooling. This is normal and does not mean that the cake is not cooked.

1. Preheat the oven to 350°F, 10 minutes before baking. Lightly grease and line the bottom of a 2-lb loaf pan. Place the orange in a small saucepan, cover with cold water and bring to a boil. Simmer for 1 hour until completely soft. Drain and let cool.

2. Place 2 egg yolks, 1 whole egg, and the sugar in a heatproof bowl set over a pan of simmering water and beat until doubled in bulk. Remove from the heat and continue to beat for 5 minutes until cooled.

3. Cut the whole orange in half and discard the seeds, then place into a food processor or blender and blend to a puree. Carefully fold the puree into the egg-yolk mixture with the ground almonds and melted chocolate.

4. Beat the egg whites until stiff peaks form. Fold a large spoonful of the egg whites into the chocolate mixture, then gently fold the remaining egg whites into the mixture.

5. Pour into the prepared pan and bake in the preheated oven for 50 minutes, or until firm and a skewer inserted into the center comes out clean. Cool in the pan before turning out of the pan and carefully discarding the lining paper.

6. Meanwhile, whip the heavy cream until just thickened. In another bowl, blend the cream cheese with the confectioners' sugar and marmalade until smooth, then fold in the heavy cream.

7. Chill the marmalade cream in the refrigerator until required. Decorate with orange zest and serve the cake cut in slices with the marmalade cream.

2

3

6

White Chocolate & Raspberry Mousse Cake

INGREDIENTS

Cuts into 8 slices

4 eggs
1/2 cup/1/4 lb superfine sugar
3/4 cup/3 oz all-purpose flour, sifted
1/4 cup/1 oz cornstarch, sifted
3 gelatin leaves
4 cups/1 lb raspberries, thawed if frozen
14 squares/14 oz white chocolate
3/4 cup/7 oz plain yogurt
2 egg whites
2 tbsp/1 oz superfine sugar
4 tbsp raspberry or orange liqueur
3/4 cup/7 fl oz heavy cream
fresh raspberries, halved, to decorate

HELPFUL HINT

Do not try to wrap the chocolate-covered parchment around the cake before it is nearly set or it will run down and be uneven.

1 Preheat the oven to 375°F, 10 minutes before baking. Grease and line 2 9-inch cake pans. Beat the eggs and sugar until thick and creamy, and the whisk leaves a trail in the mixture. Fold in the flour and cornstarch, then divide between the pans. Bake in the preheated oven for 12–15 minutes or until risen and firm. Cool in the pans, then turn out onto wire racks.

2 Place the gelatin with 4 tablespoons cold water in a dish and leave to soften for 5 minutes. Puree half the raspberries, press through a strainer, then heat until nearly boiling. Squeeze out excess water from the gelatin, add to the puree, and stir until dissolved. Set aside.

3 Melt 6 squares/6 oz of the chocolate in a bowl set over a saucepan of simmering water. Leave to cool, then stir in the yogurt and puree. Beat the egg whites until stiff and beat in the sugar. Fold into the raspberry mixture with the rest of the raspberries.

4 Line the sides of a 9-inch springform pan with nonstick baking parchment. Place 1 layer of sponge in the bottom and sprinkle with half the liqueur. Pour in the raspberry mixture and top with the second sponge. Brush with the remaining liqueur. Press down and chill in the refrigerator for 4 hours. Unmould onto a plate.

5 Cut a strip of double-thick nonstick baking parchment to fit around the cake and stand 1/2 inch higher. Melt the remaining white chocolate and spread thickly onto the parchment. Leave until just setting. Wrap around the cake and freeze for 15 minutes. Peel away the parchment. Whip the cream until thick and spread over the top of the cake. Decorate with raspberries.

1

2

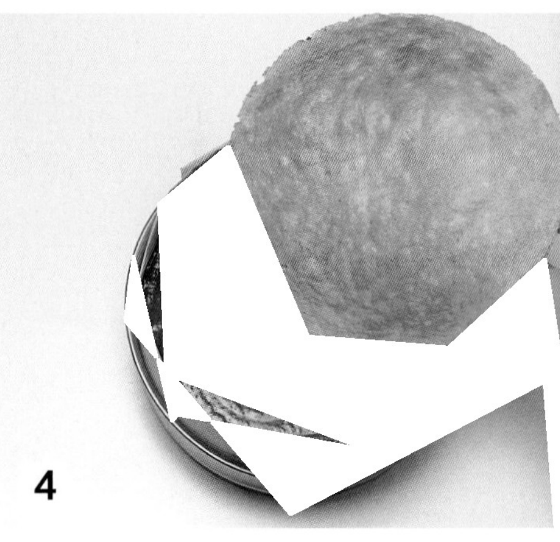

4

Chocolate Orange Fudge Cake

INGREDIENTS

Cuts into 8–10 slices

$^2/_3$ cup/$2^1/_2$ oz unsweetened cocoa
1 tbsp grated orange zest
3 cups/$^3/_4$ lb self-rising flour
2 tsp baking powder
1 tsp baking soda
$^1/_2$ tsp salt
1 cup/$^1/_2$ lb firmly packed golden brown sugar
$1^1/_2$ sticks/6 oz butter, softened
3 eggs
1 tsp vanilla extract
$1^1/_8$ cups/9 fl oz sour cream
6 tbsp butter
6 tbsp milk
rind of 1 orange, thinly pared
6 tbsp unsweetened cocoa
$2^1/_4$ cups/9 oz confectioners' sugar, sifted

1 Preheat the oven to 350°F, 10 minutes before baking. Lightly grease and line 2 9-inch, round cake pans with nonstick baking parchment. Blend the unsweetened cocoa and $^1/_4$ cup/2 fl oz boiling water until smooth. Stir in the orange zest and set aside. Sift together the flour, baking powder, baking soda, and salt, then set aside. Cream together the sugar and softened butter, and beat in the eggs, 1 at a time, then the cocoa mixture and vanilla extract. Finally, stir in the flour mixture and the sour cream in alternate spoonfuls.

2 Divide the mixture between the prepared pans and bake in the preheated oven for 35 minutes, or until the edges of the cake pull away from the pan and the tops spring back when lightly pressed. Cool in the pans for 10 minutes, then turn out onto wire racks until cold.

3 Gently heat together the butter and milk with the pared orange rind. Simmer for 10 minutes, stirring occasionally. Remove from the heat and discard the orange rind.

4 Pour the warm orange and milk mixture into a large bowl and stir in the unsweetened cocoa. Gradually beat in the sifted confectioners' sugar and beat until the frosting is smooth and spreadable. Place 1 cake onto a large serving plate. Top with about one-quarter of the frosting, place the second cake on top, then cover the cake completely with the remaining frosting. Serve.

HELPFUL HINT

This cake keeps exceptionally well in an airtight container for up to 5 days.

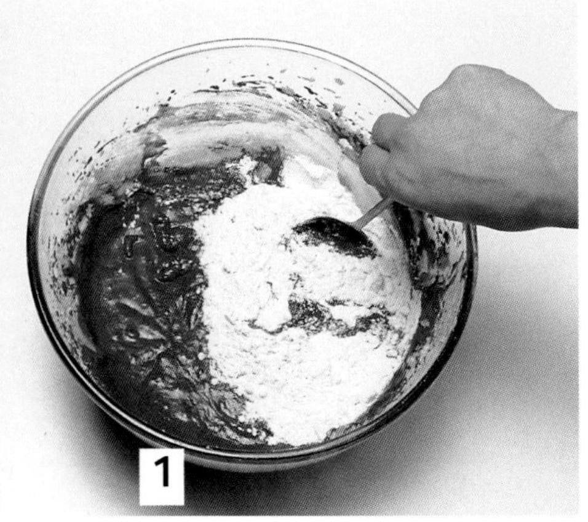
1

2

4

Cranberry & White Chocolate Cake

INGREDIENTS

Serves 4

2 sticks/½ lb butter, softened
1⅛ cups/9 oz cream cheese
⅔ cup/5 oz firmly packed golden brown sugar
1 cup/7 oz superfine sugar
3 tsp grated orange zest
1 tsp vanilla extract
4 eggs
3¼ cups/13 oz all-purpose flour
2 tsp baking powder
¾ cup/7 oz cranberries, thawed if frozen
8 squares/½ lb white chocolate, coarsely chopped
2 tbsp orange juice

1 Preheat the oven to 350°F, 10 minutes before baking. Lightly grease and flour a 9-inch fancy tube mold (kugelhopf pan) or ring mold. Using an electric mixer, cream the butter and cheese with the sugars until light and fluffy. Add the grated orange zest and vanilla extract, and beat until smooth, then beat in the eggs, 1 at a time.

2 Sift the flour and baking powder together and stir into the creamed mixture, beating well after each addition. Fold in the cranberries and 6 squares/6 oz of the white chocolate. Spoon into the prepared mold and bake in the preheated oven for 1 hour, or until firm and a skewer inserted into the center comes out clean. Cool in the mold before turning out onto on a wire rack.

3 Melt the remaining white chocolate, stir until smooth, then stir in the orange juice and let cool until thickened. Transfer the cake to a serving plate and spoon over the white chocolate and orange glaze. Let set.

TASTY TIP

If fresh or frozen cranberries are not available, substitute with a peeled and diced cooking apple, raisins, dried cranberries, or ready-to-eat chopped dried apricots.

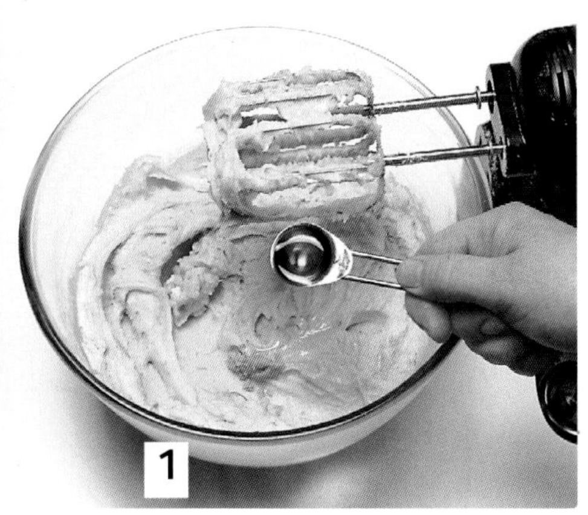
1

2

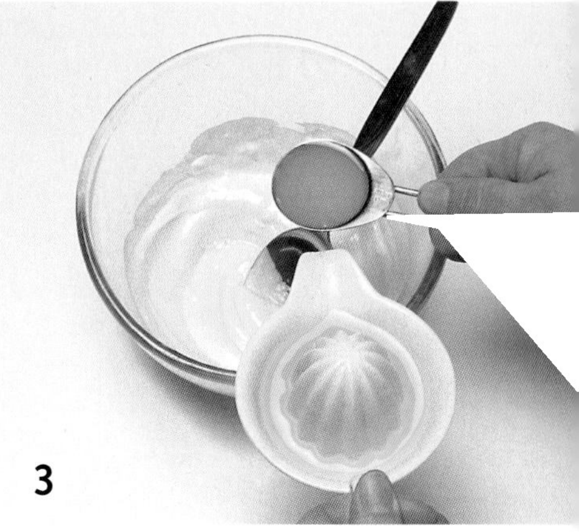
3

Fresh Strawberry Sponge Cake

INGREDIENTS

Serves 8–10

- $^{3}/_{4}$ cup/6 oz unsalted butter, softened
- $^{3}/_{4}$ cup/6 oz superfine sugar
- 1 tsp vanilla extract
- 3 eggs, beaten
- 1$^{1}/_{2}$ cups/6 oz self-rising flour
- $^{1}/_{2}$ cup/$^{1}/_{4}$ pint heavy cream
- 2 tbsp confectioners' sugar, sifted
- 1$^{1}/_{2}$ cups/$^{1}/_{2}$ lb fresh strawberries, hulled and chopped
- few extra strawberries, to decorate

HELPFUL HINT

For sponge cakes, it is important to achieve the correct consistency of the uncooked mixture. Check it after folding in the flour by tapping a spoonful of the mixture on the side of the bowl. If it drops easily, 'dropping' consistency has been reached. If it is too stiff, fold in a tablespoon of cooled boiled water.

1 Preheat the oven to 375°F, 10 minutes before baking. Lightly grease and line the bottoms of 2 8-inch, round cake pans with waxed paper or baking parchment.

2 Using an electric mixer, beat the butter, sugar, and vanilla extract until pale and fluffy. Gradually beat in the eggs, a little at a time, beating well between each addition.

3 Sift half the flour over the mixture, and using a metal spoon or rubber spatula, gently fold into the mixture. Sift over the remaining flour and fold in until just blended.

4 Divide the mixture between the pans, spreading evenly. Gently smooth the surfaces with the back of a spoon. Bake in the center of the preheated oven for 20–25 minutes, or until well risen and golden.

5 Remove and leave to cool before turning out onto a wire rack. Whip the cream with 1 tablespoon of the confectioners' sugar until it forms soft peaks. Fold in the chopped strawberries.

6 Spread 1 cake layer evenly with the mixture and top with the second cake layer, rounded side up.

7 Thickly dust the cake with confectioners' sugar and decorate with the remaining strawberries. Carefully slide onto a serving plate and serve.

2

4

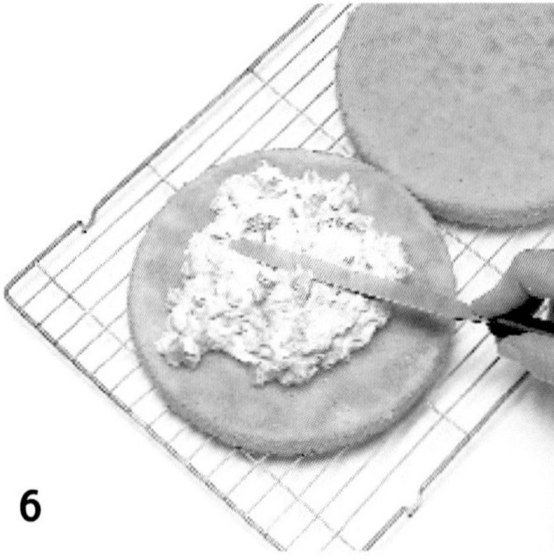
6

Almond Angel Cake with Amaretto Cream

INGREDIENTS

Cuts into 10–12 slices

1½ cups/6 oz confectioners' sugar, plus 2–3 tbsp
1¼ cups/5 oz all-purpose flour
1½ cups/12 fl oz egg whites (about 10 egg whites)
1½ tsp cream of tartar
½ tsp vanilla extract
1 tsp almond extract
¼ tsp salt
1 scant cup/7 oz superfine sugar
¾ cup/6 fl oz heavy cream
2 tbsp Amaretto liqueur
fresh raspberries, to decorate

1 Preheat the oven to 350°F, 10 minutes before baking. Sift together the 1½ cups/6 oz confectioners' sugar and flour. Stir to blend, then sift again and set aside.

2 Using an electric mixer, beat the egg whites, cream of tartar, vanilla extract, ½ teaspoon of the almond extract, and salt on medium speed until soft peaks form. Gradually add the superfine sugar, 2 tablespoons at a time, beating well after each addition, until stiff peaks form.

3 Sift about one-third of the flour mixture over the egg-white mixture, and using a metal spoon or rubber spatula, gently fold into the egg-white mixture. Repeat, folding the flour mixture into the egg-white mixture in 2 more batches. Spoon gently into an ungreased angel food cake pan or 10-inch tube pan.

4 Bake in the preheated oven until risen and golden on top and the surface springs back quickly when gently pressed with a clean finger. Immediately invert the cake pan and cool completely in the pan.

5 When cool, carefully run a sharp knife around the edge of the pan and the center ring to loosen the cake from the edge. Using the fingertips, ease the cake from the pan and invert onto a cake plate. Thickly dust the cake with the extra confectioners' sugar.

6 Whip the cream with the remaining almond extract, Amaretto liqueur, and a little more confectioners' sugar, until soft peaks form.

7 Fill a piping bag fitted with a star tip with half the cream, and pipe around the bottom edge of the cake. Decorate the edge with the fresh raspberries and serve the remaining cream separately.

FOOD FACT

Angel cake has a very light and delicate texture, and can be difficult to slice. For best results, use 2 forks gently to separate a portion of the cake.

1

3

7

White Chocolate Cheesecake

INGREDIENTS

Cuts into 16 slices

For the base:

1²/₃ cups/5 oz Graham crackers
½ cup/2 oz whole almonds, lightly toasted
½ stick/2 oz butter, melted
½ tsp almond extract

For the filling:

12 squares/¾ lb good-quality white chocolate, chopped
½ cup/4 fl oz heavy cream
3 cups/1½ lb cream cheese, softened
¼ cup/2 oz superfine sugar
4 extra-large eggs
2 tbsp Amaretto or almond-flavor liqueur

For the topping:

2 cups/¾ pint sour cream
¼ cup/2 oz superfine sugar
½ tsp almond or vanilla extract
white chocolate curls, to decorate

1 Preheat the oven to 350°F, 10 minutes before baking. Lightly grease a 9 x 3-inch springform pan. Crush the Graham crackers and almonds in a food processor to form fine crumbs. Pour in the butter and almond extract and blend. Pour the crumbs into the pan and using the back of a spoon, press onto the bottom and up the sides to within ½ inch of the top of the pan edge.

2 Bake in the preheated oven for 5 minutes to set. Remove and transfer to a wire rack. Reduce the oven temperature to 300°F.

3 Heat the white chocolate and cream in a saucepan over a low heat, stirring constantly until melted. Remove and cool.

4 Beat the cream cheese and sugar until smooth. Add the eggs, one at a time, beating well after each addition. Slowly beat in the cooled white chocolate cream and the Amaretto and pour into the baked crust. Place on a baking tray and bake for 45–55 minutes, until the edge of the cake is firm, but the center is slightly soft. Reduce the oven temperature if the top begins to brown. Remove to a wire rack and increase the temperature to 400°F.

5 To make the topping, beat the sour cream, sugar, and almond or vanilla extract until smooth, and gently pour over the cheesecake, tilting the pan to distribute the topping evenly. Alternatively spread with a metal palette knife.

6 Bake for another 5 minutes to set. Turn off the oven and leave the door halfway open for about 1 hour. Transfer to a wire rack and run a sharp knife around the edge of the crust to separate from the pan. Cool and refrigerate until chilled. Remove from the pan, decorate with white chocolate curls, and serve.

1

4

5

Italian Polenta Cake with Mascarpone Cream

INGREDIENTS

Cuts into 6–8 slices

1 tsp butter and flour for the pan
1 scant cup/3½ oz all-purpose flour
¼ cup/1½ oz polenta or yellow cornmeal
1 tsp baking powder
¼ tsp salt
grated zest of 1 lemon
2 eggs
½ cup plus 2 tbsp/5 oz superfine sugar
5 tbsp milk
½ tsp almond extract
2 tbsp golden raisins
6 tbsp/3 oz unsalted butter, softened
2 dessert pears, peeled, cored, and thinly sliced
2 tbsp apricot jelly
¼ cup/6 oz mascarpone cheese
1–2 tsp sugar
¼ cup/2 fl oz heavy cream
2 tbsp Amaretto liqueur or rum
2–3 tbsp slivered almonds, toasted
confectioners' sugar, to dust

1 Preheat the oven to 375°F, 10 minutes before baking. Butter a 9-inch springform pan. Dust lightly with flour.

2 Stir the flour, polenta or cornmeal, baking powder, salt, and lemon zest together. Beat the eggs and half the sugar until light and fluffy. Slowly beat in the milk and almond extract.

3 Stir in the raisins, then beat in the flour mixture and ½ stick/2 oz of the butter.

4 Spoon into the pan and smooth the top evenly. Arrange the pear slices on top in overlapping concentric circles.

5 Melt the remaining butter and brush over the pear slices. Sprinkle with the rest of the sugar.

6 Bake in the preheated oven for about 40 minutes, until puffed and golden and the edges of the pears are lightly caramelized. Transfer to a wire rack. Set aside to cool in the pan for 15 minutes.

7 Remove the cake from the pan. Heat the apricot jelly with 1 tablespoon water and brush over the top of the cake to glaze.

8 Beat the mascarpone cheese with the sugar to taste, the cream, and Amaretto or rum until smooth and forming a soft dropping consistency. Serve with the polenta cake.

9 When cool, sprinkle the almonds over the polenta cake and dust generously with the confectioners' sugar. Serve the cake with the liqueur-flavored mascarpone cream on the side.

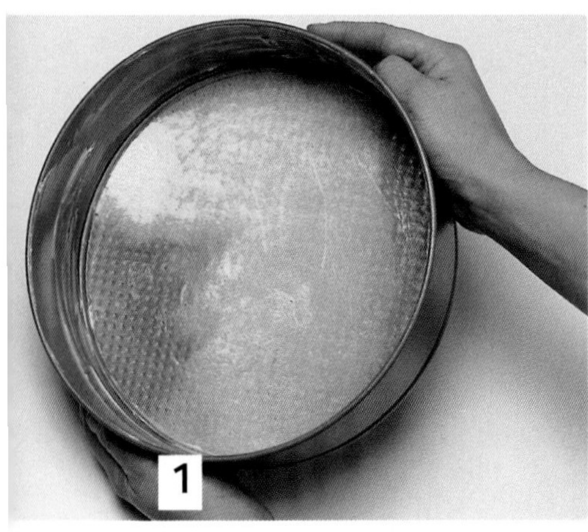
1

4

7

Autumn Apple Cake

INGREDIENTS

Cuts into 8–10 slices

- 2 cups/½ lb self-rising flour
- 1½ tsp baking powder
- ½ cup plus 2 tbsp/5 oz margarine, softened
- ¾ cup/5 oz superfine sugar, plus extra for sprinkling
- 1 tsp vanilla extract
- 2 extra-large eggs, beaten
- 2½ lbs sharp cooking apples, peeled, cored, and sliced
- 1 tbsp lemon juice
- ½ tsp ground cinnamon
- fresh custard sauce or cream, to serve

1. Preheat the oven to 325°F, 10 minutes before baking. Lightly grease and line the bottom of an 8-inch, deep cake pan with nonstick baking parchment or waxed paper. Sift the flour and baking powder into a small bowl.

2. Beat the margarine, sugar, and vanilla extract until light and fluffy. Gradually beat in the eggs a little at a time, beating well after each addition. Stir in the flour.

3. Spoon about one-third of the mixture into the pan, smoothing the surface. Toss the apple slices in the lemon juice and cinnamon, and spoon over the cake mixture, making a thick even layer. Spread the remaining mixture over the apple layer to the edge of the pan, making sure the apples are covered. Smooth the top with the back of a wet spoon and sprinkle generously with sugar.

4. Bake in the preheated oven for 1½ hours, or until well risen and golden, the apples are tender, and the center of the cake springs back when pressed lightly. (Reduce the oven temperature slightly and cover the cake loosely with kitchen foil if the top browns too quickly.)

5. Transfer to a wire rack and cool for about 20 minutes in the pan. Run a thin knife blade between the cake and the pan to loosen the cake and invert onto a paper-lined rack. Turn the cake right side up and cool. Serve with the custard sauce or cream.

FOOD FACT

Cooking apples are extremely versatile, as they can be baked, pureed, poached, and used in cakes and pies. Apples have a good soluble fiber content and are an important aid for dieters as they keep hunger pangs at bay.

3

3

5

Christmas Cranberry Chocolate Roulade

INGREDIENTS

Cuts into 12–14 slices

For the chocolate ganache frosting:

- 1¼ cups/½ pint heavy cream
- 12 squares/¾ lb semisweet chocolate, chopped
- 2 tbsp brandy (optional)

For the roulade:

- 5 extra-large eggs, separated
- 3 tbsp unsweetened cocoa, sifted, plus extra for dusting
- 1 cup/¼ lb confectioners' sugar, sifted, plus extra for dusting
- ¼ tsp cream of tartar

For the filling:

- ¾ cup/6 oz cranberry sauce
- 1-2 tbsp brandy (optional)
- ⅔ cup/¾ pint heavy cream, whipped to soft peaks

To decorate:

- candied orange strips
- dried cranberries

1 Preheat the oven to 400°F. Bring the cream to a boil over a medium heat. Remove from the heat and add all of the chocolate, stirring until melted. Stir in the brandy, if using, and strain into a medium bowl. Cool, then refrigerate for 6–8 hours.

2 Lightly grease and line a 15½ x 10½-inch jelly-roll pan with nonstick baking parchment. Using an electric mixer, beat the egg yolks until thick and creamy. Slowly beat in the unsweetened cocoa and half the confectioners' sugar and set aside. Beat the egg whites and cream of tartar into soft peaks. Gradually beat in the remaining sugar until the mixture is stiff and glossy. Gently fold the yolk mixture into the egg whites with a metal spoon or rubber spatula. Spread evenly into the pan.

3 Bake in the preheated oven for 15 minutes. Remove and invert onto a large sheet of waxed paper, dusted with unsweetened cocoa. Cut off the crisp edges of the cake, then roll up. Leave on a wire rack until cold.

4 For the filling, heat the cranberry sauce with the brandy, if using, until warm and spreadable. Unroll the cooled cake and spread with the cranberry sauce. Let cool and set. Carefully spoon the whipped cream over the surface and spread to within 1 inch of the edges. Re-roll the cake. Transfer to a cake plate or tray.

5 Allow the chocolate ganache to soften at room temperature, then beat until soft and of a spreadable consistency. Spread over the roulade and, using a fork, mark the roulade with ridges to resemble tree bark. Dust with confectioners' sugar. Decorate with the candied orange strips and dried cranberries and serve.

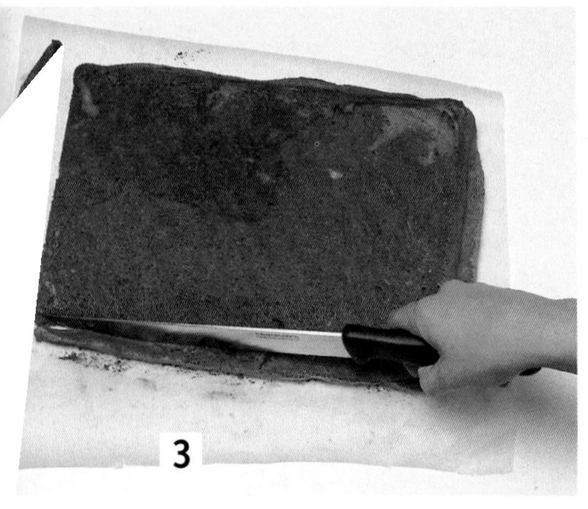
3

4

5

Buttery Passion Fruit Madeira Cake

INGREDIENTS

Cuts into 8–10 slices

2 scant cups/7½ oz all-purpose flour
1 tsp baking powder
¾ cup/6 oz sweet butter, softened
1 cup plus 2 tbsp/9 oz superfine sugar, plus 1 tsp for sprinkling
grated zest of 1 orange
1 tsp vanilla extract
3 eggs, beaten
2 tbsp milk
6 ripe passion fruits
5 tbsp/2 oz confectioners' sugar
confectioners' sugar, to dust

1 Preheat the oven to 350°F, 10 minutes before baking. Lightly grease and line the bottom of a 9 x 5-inch loaf pan with waxed paper. Sift the flour and baking powder into a bowl and set aside.

2 Beat the butter, sugar, orange zest, and vanilla extract until light and fluffy, then gradually beat in the eggs, 1 tablespoon at a time, beating well after each addition. If the mixture appears to curdle or separate, beat in a little of the flour mixture.

3 Fold in the flour mixture with the milk until just blended. Do not over mix. Spoon lightly into the prepared pan and smooth the top evenly. Sprinkle lightly with the teaspoon of superfine sugar.

4 Bake in the preheated oven for 55 minutes, or until well risen and golden brown. Remove from the oven and leave to cool for 15–20 minutes. Turn the cake out of the pan and discard the lining paper.

5 Cut the passion fruits in half and scoop out the pulp into a strainer set over a bowl. Press the juice through using a rubber spatula or wooden spoon. Stir in the confectioners' sugar and stir to dissolve, adding a little extra sugar if necessary.

6 Using a skewer, pierce holes all over the cake. Slowly spoon the passion fruit glaze over the cake and let seep in. Gently invert the cake onto a wire rack, then turn it right-side up. Dust with confectioners' sugar and cool completely. Serve the cake cold.

FOOD FACT

Regardless of its name, Madeira cake does not actually originate from the Portuguese-owned island of Madeira. It is, in fact, a traditional English favorite which acquired its name because the cake was often served with the fortified wine, Madeira.

3

5

6

Lemony Coconut Cake

INGREDIENTS

Cuts into 10–12 slices

2½ cups/10 oz all-purpose flour
2 tbsp cornstarch
1 tbsp baking powder
1 tsp salt
½ cup/5 oz shortening or soft margarine
1¼ cups/10 oz superfine sugar
grated zest of 2 lemons
1 tsp vanilla extract
3 extra-large eggs
⅔ cup/¼ pint milk
4 tbsp Malibu or rum
1-lb jar lemon curd
lime zest, to decorate

For the frosting:

1¼ cups/10 oz superfine sugar
½ cup/4 fl oz water
1 tbsp glucose
¼ tsp salt
1 tsp vanilla extract
3 extra-large egg whites
½ cup/3 oz shredded coconut

1 Preheat the oven to 350°F, 10 minutes before baking. Lightly grease and flour 2 8-inch nonstick cake pans.

2 Sift the flour, cornstarch, baking powder, and salt into a large bowl, and add the shortening or margarine, sugar, lemon zest, vanilla extract, eggs, and milk. With an electric mixer on a low speed, beat until blended, adding a little extra milk if the mixture is very stiff. Increase the speed to medium and beat for about 2 minutes.

3 Divide the mixture between the pans and smooth the tops evenly. Bake in the preheated oven for 20–25 minutes, or until the cakes feel firm and are cooked. Remove from the oven and cool before removing from the pans.

4 Put all the ingredients for the frosting, except the coconut, into a heatproof bowl placed over a saucepan of simmering water. (Do not allow the bottom of the bowl to touch the water.)

5 Using an electric mixer, blend the frosting ingredients on a low speed. Increase the speed to high and beat for 7 minutes, until the whites are stiff and glossy. Remove the bowl from the heat and continue beating until cool. Cover with plastic wrap.

6 Using a serrated knife, split the cake layers horizontally in half and sprinkle each cut surface with the Malibu or rum. Sandwich the cakes together with the lemon curd and press lightly.

7 Spread the top and sides generously with the frosting, swirling and peaking the top. Sprinkle the coconut over the top of the cake and gently press onto the sides to cover. Decorate the coconut cake with the lime zest and serve.

2

6

7

Wild Strawberry & Rose Petal Jelly Cake

INGREDIENTS

Cuts into 8 servings

- 2½ cups/10 oz all-purpose flour
- 1 tsp baking powder
- ¼ tsp salt
- ½ cup plus 2 tbsp/5 oz unsalted butter, softened
- 1 scant cup/7 oz superfine sugar
- 2 extra-large eggs, beaten
- 2 tbsp rosewater
- ½ cup/4 fl oz milk
- ½ cup/¼ lb rose petal or strawberry jelly, slightly warmed
- ¾ cup/¼ lb wild strawberries, hulled, or baby strawberries, chopped
- frosted rose petals, to decorate

For the rose cream filling:

- ¾ cup/7 fl oz heavy cream
- 1 tbsp/1 fl oz plain yogurt
- 2 tbsp rosewater
- 1–2 tbsp confectioners' sugar

1. Preheat the oven to 350°F, 10 minutes before baking. Lightly grease and flour an 8-inch nonstick cake pan. Sift the flour, baking powder, and salt into a bowl and set aside.

2. Beat the butter and sugar until light and fluffy. Beat in the eggs, a little at a time, then stir in the rosewater. Gently fold in the flour mixture and milk with a metal spoon or rubber spatula and mix lightly together.

3. Spoon the cake mixture into the pan, spreading evenly and smoothing the top.

4. Bake in the preheated oven for 25–30 minutes, or until well risen and golden and the center springs back when pressed with a clean finger. Remove and cool, then remove from the pan.

5. For the filling, beat the cream, yogurt, 1 tablespoon of the rosewater, and 1 tablespoon of the confectioners' sugar until soft peaks form. Split the cake horizontally in half and sprinkle with the remaining rosewater.

6. Spread the warmed jelly on the bottom of the cake. Top with half the whipped cream mixture, then sprinkle with half the strawberries. Place the remaining cake half on top. Spread with the remaining cream and swirl, if desired. Decorate with the rose petals. Dust the cake lightly with a little confectioners' sugar and serve.

2

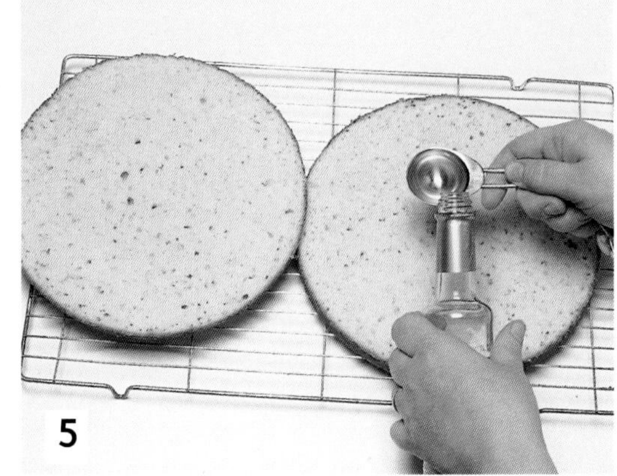
5

6

Raspberry & Hazelnut Meringue Cake

INGREDIENTS

Cuts into 8 slices

For the meringue:

4 extra-large egg whites
1/4 tsp cream of tartar
1 cup/1/2 lb superfine sugar
3/4 cup/3 oz hazelnuts, skinned, toasted, and finely ground

For the filling:

1 1/4 cups/1/2 pint heavy cream
1 tbsp confectioners' sugar
1–2 tbsp raspberry-flavored liqueur (optional)
2 1/2 cups/3/4 lb fresh raspberries

1 Preheat the oven to 275°F. Line 2 cookie sheets with nonstick baking parchment and draw an 8-inch circle on each. Beat the egg whites and cream of tartar until soft peaks form, then gradually beat in the sugar, 2 tablespoons at a time.

2 Beat well after each addition until the whites are stiff and glossy. Using a metal spoon or rubber spatula, gently fold in the ground hazelnuts.

3 Divide the mixture evenly between the 2 circles and spread neatly. Swirl 1 of the circles to make a decorative top layer. Bake in the preheated oven for about 1 1/2 hours, until crisp and dry. Turn off the oven and leave the meringues to cool for 1 hour. Transfer to a wire rack to cool completely. Carefully peel off the papers.

4 For the filling, whip the cream, confectioners' sugar, and liqueur, if using, together until soft peaks form. Place the flat round on a serving plate. Spread over most of the cream, setting aside some for decorating, and arrange the raspberries in concentric circles over the cream.

5 Place the swirly meringue on top of the cream and raspberries, pressing down gently. Pipe the remaining cream onto the meringue, decorate with a few raspberries, and serve.

HELPFUL HINT

It is essential when beating egg whites that the bowl being used is completely clean and dry, as any grease or oil will prevent the egg whites from gaining the volume needed.

2

3

4

Chocolate & Almond Daquoise with Summer Berries

INGREDIENTS

Cuts into 8 servings

For the almond meringues:

6 extra-large egg whites
1/4 tsp cream of tartar
1 cup/10 oz superfine sugar
1/2 tsp almond extract
1/2 cup/2 oz blanched or slivered almonds, lightly toasted and finely ground

For the chocolate buttercream:

6 tbsp/3 oz butter, softened
4 cups/1 lb confectioners' sugar, sifted
6 tbsp/2 oz unsweetened cocoa, sifted
3–4 tbsp milk or light cream
3 cups/1 1/4 lb mixed summer berries such as raspberries, strawberries, and blackberries

To decorate:

toasted slivered almonds
confectioners' sugar

1 Preheat the oven to 275°F, 10 minutes before baking. Line 3 cookie sheets with nonstick baking parchment and draw an 8-inch circle on each one.

2 Beat the egg whites and cream of tartar until soft peaks form. Gradually beat in the sugar, 2 tablespoons at a time, beating well after each addition, until the whites are stiff and glossy.

3 Beat in the almond extract, then using a metal spoon or rubber spatula gently fold in the ground almonds.

4 Divide the mixture evenly between the 3 circles of baking parchment, spreading neatly into the circles and smoothing the tops evenly.

5 Bake in the preheated oven for about 1 1/4 hours or until crisp, rotating the cookie sheets halfway through cooking. Turn off the oven, let cool for about 1 hour, then remove and cool completely before discarding the lining paper

6 Beat the butter, confectioners' sugar, and unsweetened cocoa until smooth and creamy, adding the milk or cream to form a soft consistency.

7 Set aside about a quarter of the berries to decorate. Spread 1 meringue with a third of the buttercream and top with a third of the remaining berries. Repeat with the other meringue circles, buttercream, and berries.

8 Sprinkle with the toasted slivered almonds, the remaining berries, and sprinkle with confectioners' sugar and serve.

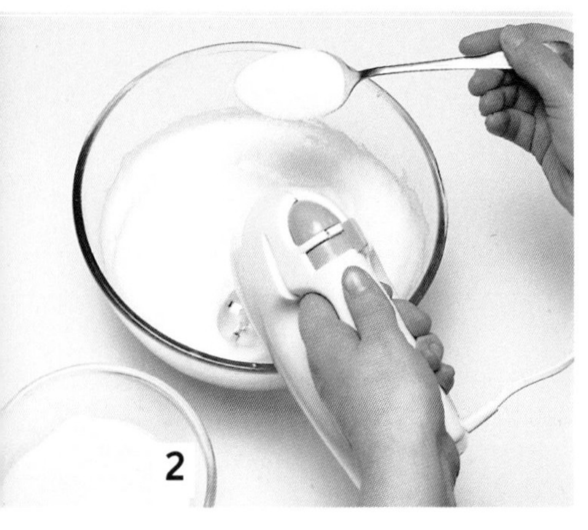
2

6

7

Orange Fruit Cake

INGREDIENTS

Cuts into 10–12 slices

For the orange cake:

2 cups/$^1/_2$ lb self-rising flour
2 tsp baking powder
1 cup/$^1/_2$ lb superfine sugar
1 cup/$^1/_2$ lb butter, softened
4 extra-large eggs
grated zest of 1 orange
2 tbsp orange juice
2–3 tbsp Cointreau or orange-flavored liqueur
1 cup/$^1/_4$ lb chopped nuts
cherries, blueberries, raspberries, and sprigs mint to decorate
confectioners' sugar, to dust (optional)

For the filling:

2 cups/$^3/_4$ pint heavy cream
$^1/_3$ cup/2 fl oz plain yogurt
$^1/_2$ tsp vanilla extract
2–3 tbsp Cointreau or orange-flavored liqueur
1 tbsp confectioners' sugar
3$^1/_2$ cups/1 lb orange fruits, such as mango, peach, nectarine, papaya, and yellow plums

1 Preheat the oven to 350°F, 10 minutes before baking. Lightly grease and line the bottom of a 10-inch tube pan or deep springform pan with nonstick baking parchment.

2 Sift the flour and baking powder into a large bowl, then stir in the sugar. Make a well in the center and add the butter, eggs, grated zest, and orange juice. Beat until blended and a smooth mixture is formed. Turn into the pan and smooth the top.

3 Bake in the preheated oven for 35–45 minutes, or until golden and the sides begin to shrink from the edge of the pan. Remove, cool before removing from the pan, and discard the lining paper.

4 Using a serrated knife, cut the cake horizontally about one-third from the top to remove the top layer. If not using a tube pan, scoop out a center ring of sponge from two thirds of both cake layers, making a hollow tunnel. Set aside for a trifle or other dessert. Sprinkle the cut sides with the Cointreau or orange-flavored liqueur.

5 For the filling, whip the cream and yogurt with the vanilla extract, Cointreau or orange-flavored liqueur, and confectioners' sugar until soft peaks form.

6 Chop the orange fruits and fold into the cream. Spoon some of this mixture onto the bottom cake layer, mounding it slightly. Transfer to a serving plate.

7 Cover with the top layer of sponge and spread the remaining cream mixture over the top and sides. Press the chopped nuts into the sides of the cake and decorate the top with the cherries, blueberries, and raspberries. If liked, dust the top with confectioners' sugar and serve.

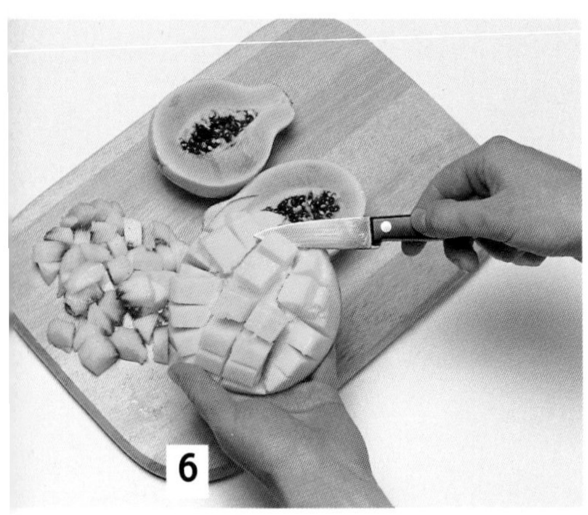
6

7

7

Chocolate Mousse Cake

INGREDIENTS

Serves 8–10

For the cake:

16 squares/1 lb unsweetened chocolate, chopped
½ cup/¼ lb butter, softened
3 tbsp brandy
9 extra-large eggs, separated
⅔ cup/5 oz superfine sugar

For the chocolate glaze:

1 cup/8 fl oz heavy cream
8 squares/½ lb unsweetened chocolate, chopped
2 tbsp brandy
1 tbsp light cream and white chocolate curls, to decorate

FOOD FACT

Wonderfully rich and delicious served with a fruity compote—why not try making cherry compote using either fresh, if in season, or otherwise canned in fruit juice. Remove the pits from the cherries, or drain and then simmer on a low heat with a little apple juice until reduced.

1 Preheat the oven to 350°F, 10 minutes before baking. Lightly grease and line the bottoms and sides of 2 8-inch springform pans with baking parchment. Melt the chocolate and butter in a bowl set over a saucepan of simmering water. Stir until smooth. Remove from the heat and stir in the brandy.

2 After setting aside 2 tablespoons of the sugar, beat the egg yolks and the sugar until thick and creamy. Slowly beat in the chocolate mixture until smooth and well blended. Beat the egg whites until soft peaks form, then sprinkle over the remaining sugar, and continue beating until stiff but not dry.

3 Gently fold the egg whites into the chocolate mixture. Divide about two thirds of the mixture evenly between the pans, tapping to distribute the mixture evenly. Set aside the remaining one third of the chocolate mousse mixture for the filling. Bake in the preheated oven for about 20 minutes, or until the cakes are well risen and set. Remove and cool for at least 1 hour.

4 Loosen the edges of the cake layers with a knife. Using the fingertips, lightly press the crusty edges down. Pour the rest of the mousse over one layer, spreading until even. Carefully unclip the side of the other pan and remove the other cake. Gently invert onto the mousse, bottom side up to make a flat top layer. Discard lining paper and chill for 4–6 hours, or until set.

5 To make the glaze, melt the cream and chocolate with the brandy in a heavy-based saucepan and stir until smooth. Cool until thickened. Unclip the side of the mousse cake and place on a wire rack. Pour over half the glaze and spread to cover. Let set, then decorate with chocolate curls. To serve, heat the remaining glaze, pour it around each slice, and dot with cream.

1

2

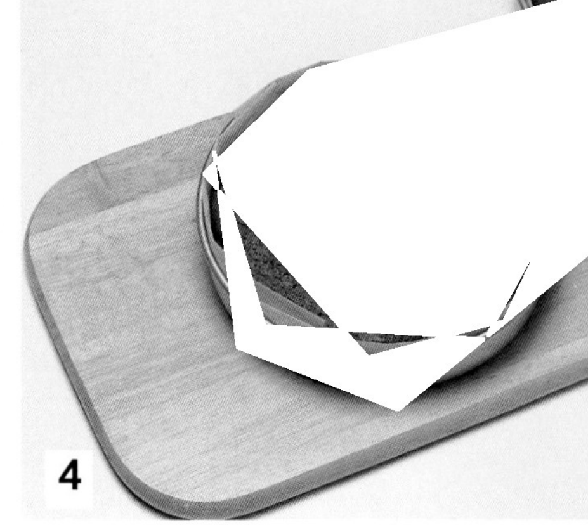
4

Desserts

These recipes extend from the simplistic to the sophisticated and can thus provide the perfect conclusion to a range of occasions. From family favorites such as Jam Roly Poly and Crunchy Rhubarb Crisp to luxurious choices such as Chocolate Raspberry Pastry, there is something to satisfy everyone.

Iced Chocolate & Raspberry Mousse

INGREDIENTS

Serves 4

12 ladyfingers
juice of 2 oranges
2 tbsp orange-flavored liqueur
1 cup/½ pint heavy cream
6 squares/6 oz unsweetened chocolate, broken into small pieces
2 cups/½ lb frozen raspberries
6 tbsp confectioners' sugar, sifted
unsweetened cocoa, for dusting

To decorate:

few fresh whole raspberries
few leaves mint
grated white chocolate

1 Break the ladyfingers into small pieces and divide between 4 individual glass dishes. Blend together the orange juice and orange-flavored liqueur, then drizzle evenly over the ladyfingers. Cover with plastic wrap and chill in the refrigerator for 30 minutes.

2 Meanwhile, place the cream in a small, heavy-based saucepan and heat gently, stirring occasionally until boiling. Remove the saucepan from the heat then add the pieces of unsweetened chocolate and leave to stand untouched for about 7 minutes. Using a whisk, beat the chocolate and cream together, until the chocolate has melted and is well blended and completely smooth. Leave to cool slightly.

3 Place the frozen raspberries and confectioners' sugar into a food processor or blender and blend until roughly crushed.

4 Fold the crushed raspberries into the cream and chocolate mixture and mix lightly until well blended. Spoon the mousse over the chilled ladyfingers. Lightly dust with a little cocoa and decorate with whole raspberries, mint leaves, and grated white chocolate. Serve immediately.

HELPFUL HINT

Remove the raspberries from the freezer about 20 minutes before you need to puree them. This will soften them slightly but they will still be frozen.

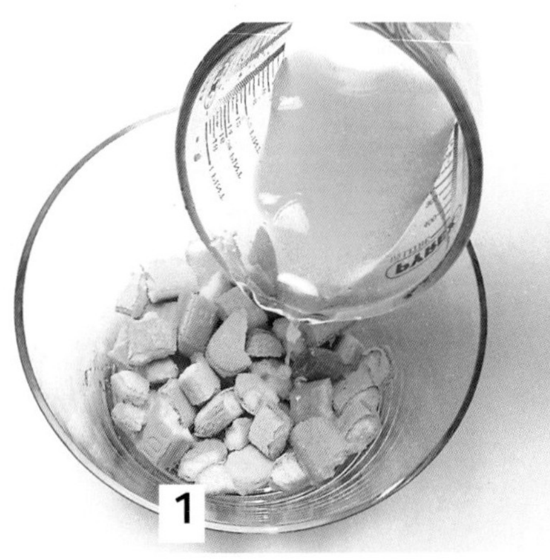
1

2

3

Chocolate Fudge Sundae

INGREDIENTS

Serves 2

For the chocolate fudge sauce:

3 squares/3 oz unsweetened chocolate, broken into pieces
1 3/4 cups/3/4 pint heavy cream
3/4 cup/6 oz unrefined superfine sugar
1/4 cup/1 oz all-purpose flour
pinch salt
1 tbsp/1/2 oz unsalted butter
1 tsp vanilla extract

For the sundae:

1 cup/1/4 lb raspberries, fresh or thawed if frozen
4 scoops vanilla ice cream
2 scoops homemade chocolate ice cream (see page 118)
2 tbsp toasted slivered almonds
a few wafers, to serve

1. To make the chocolate fudge sauce, place the chocolate and cream in a heavy-based saucepan and heat gently until the chocolate has melted into the cream. Stir until smooth. Mix the sugar with the flour and salt, then stir in sufficient chocolate mixture to make a smooth paste.

2. Gradually blend the remaining melted chocolate mixture into the paste, then pour into a clean saucepan. Cook over a low heat, stirring frequently until smooth and thick. Remove from the heat and add the butter and vanilla extract. Stir until smooth, then cool slightly.

3. To make the sundae, crush the raspberries lightly with a fork (or leave whole if preferred) and set aside. Spoon a little of the chocolate sauce into the bottom of 2 sundae glasses. Add a layer of raspberries, then a scoop each of vanilla and chocolate ice cream.

4. Pour over the sauce, sprinkle over the almonds, and serve with a wafer.

HELPFUL HINT

Ice cream will keep for 2 months in the freezer at a temperature of 0.4°F. If using homemade ice cream, let soften in the refrigerator before using.

2

3

3

Chocolate Ice Cream

INGREDIENTS

Makes 4 cups/ 1$^3/_4$ pints

2 cups/$^3/_4$ pint light cream
7 squares/7 oz unsweetened chocolate
2 eggs
2 egg yolks
$^1/_2$ cup/$^1/_4$ lb superfine sugar
1 tsp vanilla extract
1 cup/$^1/_2$ pint heavy cream

To serve:

chopped nuts
coarsely grated white and bittersweet chocolate
a few cape gooseberries or cherries

1 Set the freezer to rapid freeze, 2 hours before freezing. Place the light cream and chocolate in a heavy-based saucepan, and heat gently until the chocolate has melted. Stir until smooth. Take care not to let the mixture boil. Remove from the heat.

2 Beat the eggs, egg yolks, and all but 1 tablespoon of the sugar together in a bowl until thick and pale.

3 Beat the warmed light-cream and chocolate mixture with the vanilla extract into the custard mixture. Place the bowl over a saucepan of simmering water and continue beating until the mixture thickens and will coat the back of a spoon. To test, lift the spoon out of the mixture and draw a clean finger through the mixture coating the spoon. If it leaves a clean line, then it is ready.

4 Stand the bowl in cold water to cool. Sprinkle the surface with the remaining sugar to prevent a skin forming while it is cooling. Whip the heavy cream until soft peaks form, then beat into the cooled chocolate custard.

5 Turn the ice cream mixture into a rigid plastic container and freeze for 1 hour. Beat the ice cream thoroughly with a wooden spoon to break up all the ice crystals, then return to the freezer.

6 Continue to freeze the ice cream for a further hour, then remove and beat again. Repeat this process once or twice more, then leave the ice cream in the freezer until firm. Leave to soften in the refrigerator for at least 30 minutes before serving.

7 Remove from the refrigerator, sprinkle over the chopped nuts and grated chocolate, and serve with cape gooseberries or cherries. Turn the freezer back to its normal setting.

HELPFUL HINT

When beating the ice cream, expect it to melt a little. This is what should happen. Beating is necessary to break down any large ice crystals that have formed so that the finished ice cream is smooth rather than grainy or icy.

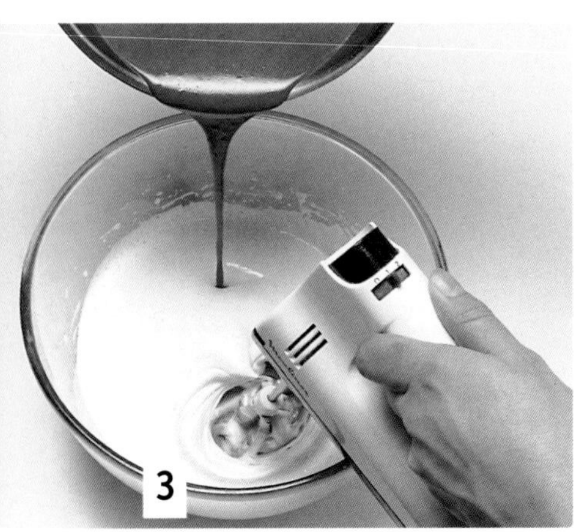
3

4

4

White Chocolate Terrine with Red Fruit Compote

INGREDIENTS

Serves 8

8 squares/$\frac{1}{2}$ lb white chocolate
1 cup/$\frac{1}{2}$ pint heavy cream
1 cup/$\frac{1}{2}$ lb full-fat soft cream cheese
2 tbsp orange rind, finely grated
$\frac{2}{3}$ cup/$\frac{1}{4}$ lb superfine sugar
3 cups/$\frac{3}{4}$ lb mixed summer fruits, such as strawberries, blueberries, and raspberries
1 tbsp orange-flavored liqueur
sprigs fresh mint, to decorate

HELPFUL HINT

Pour some boiled water into a tall jug and dip your knife into it for a few seconds. Dry the knife and use to slice the terrine, repeating the dipping when necessary.

1 Set the freezer to rapid freeze at least 2 hours before required. Lightly grease and line a 1-lb loaf pan with plastic wrap, taking care to keep the plastic wrap as wrinkle free as possible. Break the white chocolate into small pieces and place in a heatproof bowl set over a saucepan of gently simmering water. Leave for 20 minutes or until melted, then remove from the heat and stir until smooth. Let cool.

2 Whip the cream until soft peaks form. Beat the cream cheese until soft and creamy, then beat in the grated orange rind and $\frac{1}{4}$ cup/2 oz of the superfine sugar. Mix well, then fold in the whipped cream and then the cooled melted white chocolate.

3 Spoon the mixture into the prepared loaf pan and level the surface. Place in the freezer and freeze for at least 4 hours or until frozen. Once frozen, remember to return the freezer to its normal setting.

4 Place the fruits with the remaining sugar in a heavy-based saucepan and heat gently, stirring occasionally, until the sugar has dissolved and the juices from the fruits are just beginning to run. Add the orange-flavored liqueur.

5 Dip the loaf pan into hot water for 30 seconds and invert onto a serving plate. Carefully remove the pan and plastic wrap. Decorate with sprigs of mint and serve sliced with the prepared red fruit compote.

2

3

4

Chocolate Fruit Tiramisu

INGREDIENTS

Serves 4

2 ripe passion fruit
2 fresh nectarines or peaches
$^{1}/_{4}$ cup/3 oz ladyfingers
1 cup/$^{1}/_{4}$ lb amaretti cookies
5 tbsp amaretti liqueur
6 tbsp prepared black coffee
1 cup/9 oz mascarpone cheese
2 cups/$^{3}/_{4}$ pint fresh custard sauce
7 squares/7 oz unsweetened chocolate, finely chopped or grated
2 tbsp unsweetened cocoa, sifted

FOOD FACT

Mascarpone cheese is an Italian full-fat cream cheese with a very thick, creamy texture and flavor. It is a classic ingredient of tiramisu. Here, it is mixed with some ready-made custard, which gives it a lighter texture.

1 Cut the passion fruit, scoop out the seeds, and set aside. Plunge the nectarines or peaches into boiling water and leave for 2–3 minutes. Carefully remove the nectarines from the water, cut in half, and remove the pits. Peel off the skin, chop the flesh finely, and set aside.

2 Break the ladyfingers and amaretti cookies in half. Place the amaretti liqueur and prepared black coffee into a shallow dish and stir well. Place half the ladyfingers and amaretti cookies into the amaretti and coffee mixture and soak for 30 seconds.

3 Lift out both cookies from the liqueur and arrange in the bottoms of 4 deep individual glass dishes.

4 Cream the mascarpone cheese until soft and creamy, then slowly beat in the fresh custard sauce and mix well together.

5 Spoon half the mascarpone mixture over the cookies in the dishes and sprinkle with $^{1}/_{4}$ lb of the finely chopped or grated chocolate.

6 Arrange half the passion fruit seeds and the chopped nectarine or peaches over the chocolate and sprinkle with half the cocoa.

7 Place the remaining cookies in the remaining coffee liqueur mixture and soak for 30 seconds, then arrange on top of the fruit and unsweetened cocoa. Top with the remaining chopped or grated chocolate, nectarine or peach, and the mascarpone cheese mixture, piling the mascarpone high in the dishes.

8 Chill in the refrigerator for 1$^{1}/_{2}$ hours, then spoon the remaining passion fruit seeds and unsweetened cocoa over the desserts. Chill in the refrigerator for 30 minutes and serve.

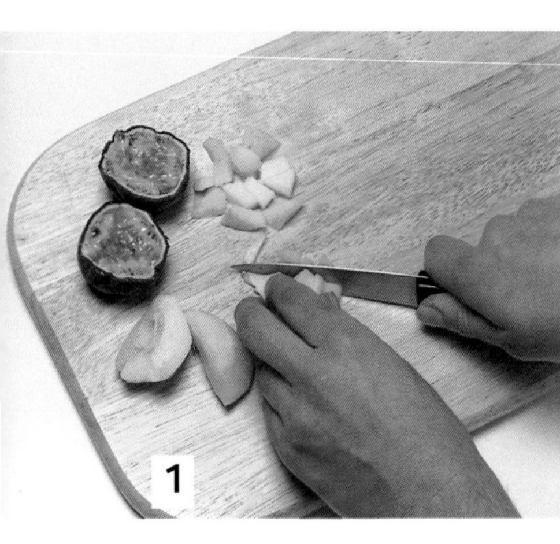
1

2

3

Crème Brûlée with Sugared Raspberries

INGREDIENTS

Serves 6

2½ cups/1 pint fresh whipping cream
4 egg yolks
⅓ cup/3 oz superfine sugar
½ tsp vanilla extract
2 tbsp/1 oz brown sugar
1 generous cup/6 oz fresh raspberries

HELPFUL HINT

Most chefs use blow torches to brown the sugar in step 7, as this is the quickest way to caramelize the top of the dessert. Take great care if using a blow torch, especially when lighting. Otherwise use the broiler, making sure that it is very hot and the dessert is thoroughly chilled before caramelizing the sugar topping. This will prevent the custard underneath from melting.

1 Preheat the oven to 300°F. Pour the cream into a bowl and place over a saucepan of gently simmering water. Heat gently but do not let boil.

2 Meanwhile, beat together the egg yolks, 4 tbsp/2 oz of the superfine sugar and the vanilla extract. When the cream is warm, pour it over the egg mixture, briskly beating until it is mixed completely.

3 Pour into 6 individual ramekin dishes and place in a roasting pan.

4 Fill the pan with enough water to come halfway up the sides of the dishes.

5 Bake in the preheated oven for about 1 hour, or until the desserts are set. (To test if set, carefully insert a round-bladed knife into the center, if the knife comes out clean, they are set.)

6 Remove the desserts from the roasting pan and let cool. Chill in the refrigerator, preferably overnight.

7 Sprinkle the sugar over the top of each dish and place the desserts under a preheated hot broiler.

8 When the sugar has caramelized and turned deep brown, remove from the heat and cool. Chill the desserts in the refrigerator for 2–3 hours before serving.

9 Toss the raspberries in the remaining superfine sugar and sprinkle over the top of each dish. Serve with a little extra cream if liked.

2

5

7

Chocolate Trifle

INGREDIENTS

Serves 4

1½ homemade or bought chocolate jelly rolls
4 tbsp strawberry jelly
3 tbsp medium sherry
3 tbsp brandy
3 cups/¾ lb fresh strawberries
2 small mangos, peeled, pitted, and diced
7 squares/7 oz unsweetened chocolate
2 tbsp custard powder
2 tbsp superfine sugar
1¼ cups/½ pint whole milk
1 cup/9 oz mascarpone cheese
1 cup/½ pint heavy cream
3 tbsp/½ oz slivered almonds, toasted

1 Slice the chocolate jelly roll thickly and spread each slice with a little strawberry jelly. Place the jelly roll slices in the bottom of a trifle dish or glass bowl. Sprinkle over the sherry and brandy and let stand for 10 minutes to let the sherry and brandy soak into the jelly roll. Slice half the strawberries and scatter evenly over the jelly roll with half the diced mangos.

2 Break the chocolate into small pieces and place in a small heatproof bowl set over a saucepan of gently simmering water. Heat gently, stirring occasionally, until the chocolate has melted and is smooth and free from lumps.

3 Blend the custard powder, sugar, and milk to a smooth paste in a bowl, then pour into a heavy-based saucepan. Place over a gentle heat and cook, stirring constantly, until the custard is smooth and thick. Add the melted chocolate and stir until smooth and blended. Remove from the heat and leave to cool. Stir in the mascarpone cheese.

4 Spoon the chocolate custard mixture over the fruit and chill in the refrigerator for 1 hour. Whip the cream until soft peaks form and pile over the top of the set custard. Sprinkle over the toasted, slivered almonds and decorate with the remaining whole strawberries and diced mango.

TASTY TIP

If you prefer, use fresh custard. Heat gently, then stir in the chocolate and mascarpone cheese. Omit the custard powder, sugar, and milk.

1

3

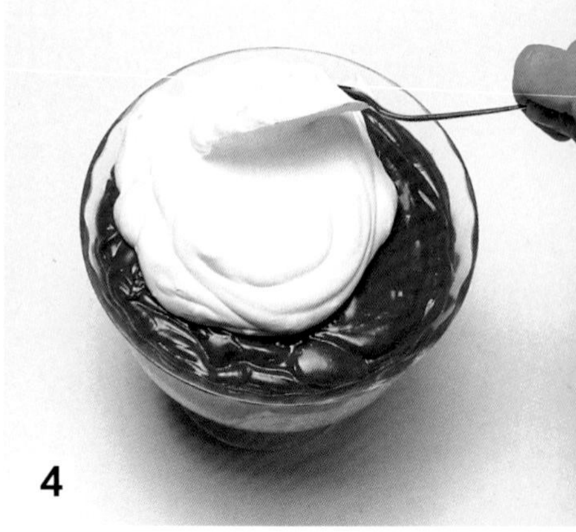
4

Chocolate Cream Puffs

INGREDIENTS

Serves 4

For the dough:

2/3 cup/1/4 pint water
1/2 stick/2 oz butter
9 tbsp/2 1/2 oz all-purpose flour, sifted
2 eggs, lightly beaten

For the custard:

1/4 cups/1/2 pint milk
pinch freshly grated nutmeg
3 egg yolks
1/4 cup/2 oz superfine sugar
2 tbsp all-purpose flour, sifted
2 tbsp cornstarch, sifted

For the sauce:

3/4 cup/6 oz firmly packed soft brown sugar
2/3 cup/1/4 pint boiling water
1 tsp instant coffee
1 tbsp unsweetened cocoa
1 tbsp brandy
3/4 stick/3 oz butter
1 tbsp corn syrup

1 Preheat the oven to 425°F, 15 minutes before baking. Lightly grease 2 cookie sheets. For the dough, place the water and the butter in a heavy-based saucepan and bring to a boil. Remove from the heat and beat in the flour. Return to the heat and cook for 1 minute or until the mixture forms a ball in the center of the saucepan.

2 Remove from the heat and leave to cool slightly, then gradually beat in the eggs a little at a time, beating well after each addition. Once all the eggs have been added, beat until the mixture is smooth and glossy. Pipe or spoon 20 small balls onto the cookie sheets, allowing plenty of room for expansion.

3 Bake in the preheated oven for 25 minutes or until well risen and golden brown. Reduce the oven temperature to 350°F. Make a hole in each ball and continue to bake for a further 5 minutes. Remove from the oven and let cool.

4 For the custard, place the milk and nutmeg in a heavy-based saucepan and bring to a boil. In another saucepan, beat together the egg yolks, sugar, and the flours, then beat in the hot milk. Bring to a boil and simmer, beating constantly for 2 minutes. Cover and let cool.

5 Spoon the custard into the profiteroles and arrange on a large serving dish. Place all the sauce ingredients in a small saucepan and bring to a boil, then simmer for 10 minutes. Remove from the heat and cool slightly before serving with the chocolate puffs.

1

2

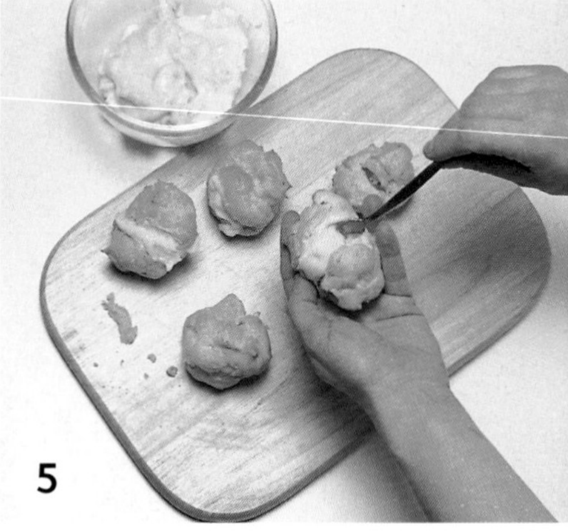
5

White Chocolate Eclairs

INGREDIENTS

Serves 4–6

½ stick/2 oz unsalted butter
⅔ cup/2½ oz all-purpose flour, sifted
2 eggs, lightly beaten
6 ripe passion fruit
1 cup/½ pint heavy cream
3 tbsp kirsch
1 tbsp confectioners' sugar
4 squares/¼ lb white chocolate, broken into pieces

1 Preheat the oven to 375°F, 10 minutes before baking. Lightly grease a cookie sheet. Place the butter and ⅔ cup/¼ pint water in a saucepan and heat until the butter has melted, then bring to a boil.

2 Remove the saucepan from the heat and immediately add the flour all at once, beating with a wooden spoon until the mixture forms a ball in the center of the saucepan. Leave to cool for 3 minutes.

3 Add the eggs a little at a time, beating well after each addition until the paste is smooth, shiny, and of a piping consistency. Spoon the mixture into a piping bag fitted with a plain tip. Sprinkle the greased cookie sheet with water. Pipe the mixture onto the cookie sheet in 3-inch lengths, using a knife to cut each pastry length neatly.

4 Bake in the preheated oven for 18–20 minutes, or until well risen and golden. Make a slit along the side of each eclair, to let the steam escape. Return the eclairs to the oven for a further 2 minutes to dry out. Transfer to a wire rack and leave to cool.

5 Halve the passion fruit, and using a small spoon, scoop the pulp of 4 of the fruits into a bowl. Add the cream, kirsch, and confectioners' sugar and whip until the cream holds it shape. Carefully spoon or pipe into the eclairs.

6 Melt the chocolate in a small heatproof bowl set over a saucepan of simmering water and stir until smooth.

7 Leave the chocolate to cool slightly, then spread over the top of the eclairs. Scoop the seeds and pulp out of the remaining passion fruit. Strain. Use the juice to drizzle around the eclairs when serving.

HELPFUL HINT

Passion fruit are readily available in supermarkets. They are small, round, purplish fruits that should have quite wrinkled skins. Smooth passion fruit are not ripe and will have little juice or flavor.

2

4

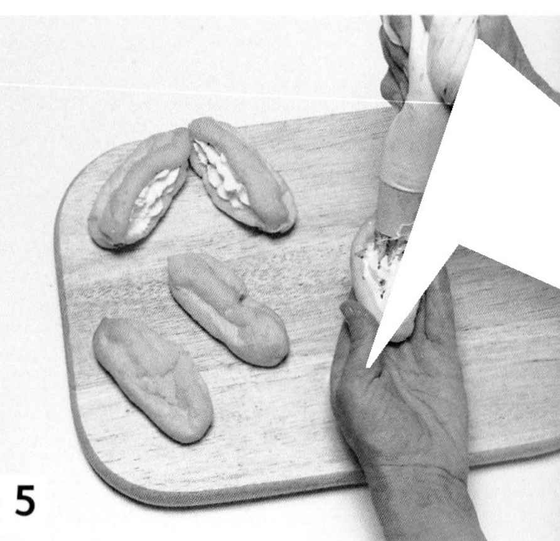
5

Chocolate & Rum Truffles

INGREDIENTS

Makes 44

For the chocolate truffles:

- 8 squares/½ lb unsweetened chocolate
- ¼ stick/1 oz butter, softened
- 2 egg yolks
- 2 tsp brandy or kirsch
- 2 tsp heavy cream
- 24 maraschino cherries, drained
- 2 tbsp unsweetened cocoa, sifted

For the rum truffles:

- 4 squares/¼ lb unsweetened chocolate
- 2 tbsp rum
- ½ cup/4 fl oz heavy cream
- ½ cup/2 oz almonds, ground
- 2 tbsp confectioners' sugar, sifted

TASTY TIP

These truffles are so easy to make, they are great to give as gifts. Roll some in confectioners' sugar, as above, and roll others in cocoa. Arrange in a gift box in a checkerboard pattern.

1 For the chocolate truffles, break the chocolate into pieces and place in a heatproof bowl set over a saucepan of gently simmering water. Leave for 20 minutes or until the chocolate has melted. Stir until the chocolate is smooth and remove from the heat. Let stand for about 6 minutes.

2 Beat the butter, egg yolks, brandy or kirsch, and heavy cream together until smooth. Stir the melted chocolate into the butter and egg-yolk mixture and stir until thick. Cover and let cool for about 30 minutes. Chill in the refrigerator for 1½ hours or until firm.

3 Divide the truffle mixture into 24 pieces and mold around the drained cherries. Roll in the unsweetened cocoa until evenly coated. Place the truffles in petit-four paper cases and chill in the refrigerator for 2 hours before serving.

4 To make the rum truffles, break the chocolate into small pieces and place in a heavy-based saucepan with the cream and rum. Heat gently until the chocolate has melted, then stir until smooth. Stir in the ground almonds, pour into a small bowl, and chill in the refrigerator for at least 6 hours or until the mixture is thick.

5 Remove the truffle mixture from the refrigerator and shape small spoonfuls, about the size of a cherry, into balls. Roll in the sifted confectioners' sugar and place in petit-four paper cases. Store the truffles in the refrigerator until ready to serve.

1

2

3

Chocolate Meringue Nest with Fruity Filling

INGREDIENTS

Serves 8

1 cup/$^{1}/_{4}$ lb hazelnuts, toasted
$^{1}/_{2}$ cup/$^{1}/_{4}$ lb superfine sugar
3 squares/3 oz unsweetened chocolate, broken into pieces
2 egg whites
pinch salt
1 tsp cornstarch
$^{1}/_{2}$ tsp white wine vinegar
chocolate curls, to decorate

For the filling:

$^{1}/_{2}$ cup/$^{1}/_{4}$ pint heavy cream
$^{2}/_{3}$ cup/5 oz mascarpone cheese
prepared summer fruits, such as strawberries, raspberries, and redcurrants

HELPFUL HINT

To make chocolate curls, melt the chocolate over hot water then pour onto a cool surface. Leave until just set but not hard, then using a large cook's knife or a cheese parer, push the blade at an angle across the surface of the chocolate to form curls.

1 Preheat the oven to 225°F, 5 minutes before baking and line a cookie sheet with nonstick baking parchment. Place the hazelnuts and 2 tablespoons of the superfine sugar in a food processor and blend to a powder. Add the chocolate and blend again until the chocolate is coarsely chopped.

2 In a clean, grease-free bowl, beat the egg whites and salt until soft peaks form. Gradually beat in the remaining sugar, a teaspoonful at a time, and continue to beat until the meringue is stiff and shiny. Fold in the cornstarch and the white wine vinegar with the chocolate and hazelnut mixture.

3 Spoon the mixture into 8 mounds, about 4 inches in diameter, on the baking parchment. Do not worry if they are not perfect shapes. Make a hollow in each mound, then place in the preheated oven. Cook for 1$^{1}/_{2}$ hours, then switch the oven off and leave in the oven until cool.

4 To make the filling, whip the cream until soft peaks form. In another bowl, beat the mascarpone cheese until it is softened, then mix with the cream. Spoon the mixture into the meringue nests and top with the fresh fruits. Decorate with a few chocolate curls and serve.

1

2

3

Chocolate Mallow Pie

INGREDIENTS

Serves 6

$1^3/_4$ cups /7 oz Graham crackers (about 18)
$^3/_4$ stick/3 oz butter, melted
6 squares/6 oz unsweetened chocolate
20 marshmallows
1 egg, separated
1 cup/$^1/_2$ pint heavy cream

1 Place the Graham crackers in a plastic bag and finely crush with a rolling pin. Alternatively, place in a food processor and blend until fine crumbs are formed.

2 Melt the butter in a medium-sized saucepan, add the crushed Graham crackers and mix together. Press into the bottom of the prepared pan and let cool in the refrigerator.

3 Melt 4 squares/$^1/_4$ lb of the chocolate with the marshmallows and 2 tablespoons water in a saucepan over a gentle heat, stirring constantly. Leave to cool slightly, then stir in the egg yolk, beat well, then return to the refrigerator until cool.

4 Beat the egg white until stiff and standing in peaks, then fold into the chocolate mixture.

5 Lightly whip the cream and fold three-quarters of the cream into the chocolate mixture. Set the remainder aside. Spoon the chocolate cream into the flan case and chill in the refrigerator until set.

6 When ready to serve, spoon the remaining cream over the chocolate pie, swirling in a decorative pattern. Grate the remaining dark chocolate and sprinkle over the cream, then serve.

TASTY TIP

Replace the Graham crackers with an equal weight of chocolate-covered Graham crackers to make a quick change to this recipe.

2

3

5

Lattice Treacle Tart

INGREDIENTS

Serves 4

For the dough:

1½ cups/6 oz all-purpose flour
3 tbsp/1½ oz butter
3 tbsp/1½ oz shortening

For the filling:

¾ cup/½ lb corn syrup
finely grated rind and juice of 1 lemon
1½ cups/3 oz fresh white bread crumbs
1 medium egg, beaten

1 Preheat the oven to 375°F. Make the dough by placing the flour, butter, and shortening in a food processor. Blend in short, sharp bursts until the mixture resembles fine bread crumbs. Remove from the processor and place in a large bowl.

2 Stir in enough cold water to make a dough and knead in a large bowl or on a floured surface until smooth and pliable.

3 Roll out the dough and use to line an 8-inch loose-bottomed fluted flan dish or pan. Set aside the dough trimmings for decoration. Chill for 30 minutes.

4 Meanwhile, to make the filling, place the corn syrup in a saucepan and warm gently with the lemon rind and juice. Tip the breadcrumbs into the tart shell and pour the syrup mixture over the top.

5 Roll the dough trimmings out on a lightly floured surface and cut into 6–8 thin strips. Lightly dampen the edge of the tart, then place the strips across the filling in a lattice pattern. Brush the ends of the strips with water and seal to the edge of the tart. Brush a little beaten egg over the dough and bake in the preheated oven for a 25 minutes, or until the filling is just set. Serve hot or cold.

TASTY TIP

Why not replace the bread crumbs with the same amount of dried coconut?

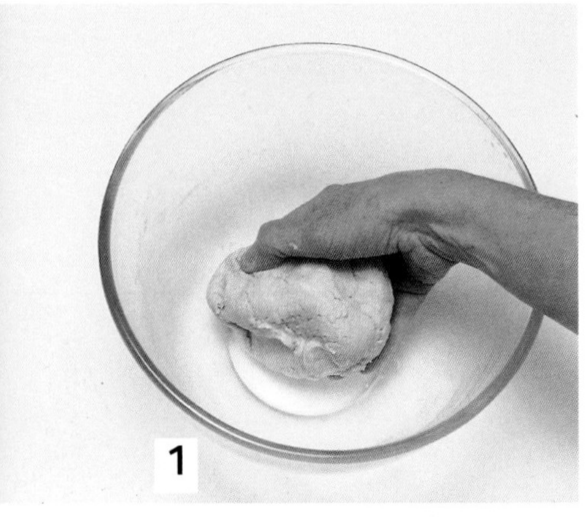
1

4

5

Chocolate, Orange & Pine Nut Tart

INGREDIENTS

Cuts into 8–10 slices

For the sweet pie crust:

- 1¼ cups/5 oz all-purpose flour
- ½ tsp salt
- 3–4 tbsp confectioners' sugar
- 1 stick/¼ lb unsalted butter, diced
- 2 egg yolks, beaten
- ½ tsp vanilla extract

For the filling:

- 4 squares/¼ lb unsweetened chocolate, chopped
- ⅔ cup/2½ oz pine nuts, lightly toasted
- 2 extra-large eggs
- grated zest of 1 orange
- 1 tbsp Cointreau or orange-flavored liqueur
- 1 cup/8 fl oz heavy cream
- 2 tbsp orange marmalade

1 Preheat the oven to 400°F, 15 minutes before baking. Place the flour, salt, and sugar in a food processor with the butter and blend briefly. Add the egg yolks, 2 tablespoons iced water, and the vanilla extract and blend until a soft dough is formed. Remove and knead until smooth, wrap in plastic wrap, and chill in the refrigerator for 1 hour.

2 Lightly grease a 9-inch springform flan pan. Roll the dough out on a lightly floured surface to an 11-inch circle and use to line the pan. Press into the sides of the flan pan, crimp the edges, prick the bottom with a fork, and chill in the refrigerator for 1 hour. Bake blind in the preheated oven for 10 minutes. Remove and place on a cookie sheet. Reduce the oven temperature to 375°F.

3 To make the filling, sprinkle the chocolate and the pine nuts evenly over the bottom of the pie crust. Beat the eggs, orange zest, Cointreau or orange-flavored liqueur, and cream in a bowl until well blended, then pour over the chocolate and pine nuts.

4 Bake in the oven for 30 minutes, or until the dough is golden and the custard mixture is just set. Transfer to a wire rack to cool slightly. Heat the marmalade with 1 tablespoon water and brush over the tart. Serve warm or at room temperature.

FOOD FACT

Cointreau is an orange-flavored liqueur and is used in many recipes. You could substitute Grand Marnier or any other orange liqueur, if you prefer.

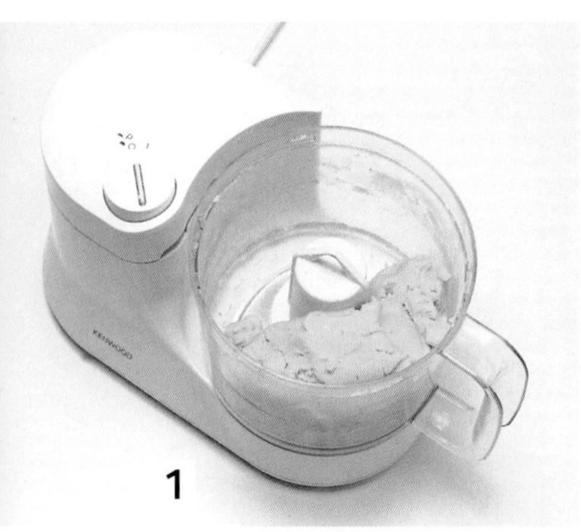
1

2

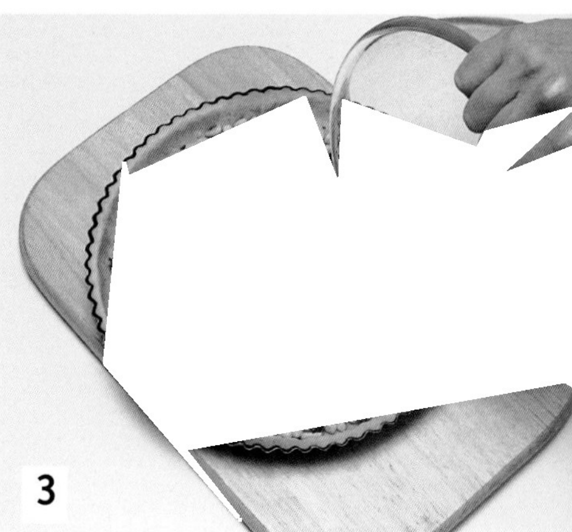
3

Chocolate Pecan Pie

INGREDIENTS

Cuts into 8–10 slices

1 cup/½ lb prepared pie crust dough (see page 140)
1¾ cups/7 oz pecan halves
4 squares/¼ lb unsweetened chocolate, chopped
¼ stick/1 oz butter, diced
3 eggs
½ cup/¼ lb light brown sugar
½ cup/6 oz corn syrup
2 tsp vanilla extract
vanilla ice cream, to serve

HELPFUL HINT

Store chocolate in a cool, dark, dry place. The best temperature to store it is 68°F—if warmer the chocolate will sweat.

HELPFUL HINT

The piecrust in this recipe is not baked blind, but the pie does not become soggy because of the long cooking time, which allows the dough to become crisp.

1 Preheat the oven to 350°F, 10 minutes before baking. Roll the prepared dough out on a lightly floured surface and use to line a 10-inch pie plate. Roll the trimmings out and use to make a decorative edge around the pie, then chill in the refrigerator for 1 hour.

2 Set aside about 60 perfect pecan halves, or enough to cover the top of the pie, then coarsely chop the remainder and set aside. Melt the chocolate and butter in a small saucepan over a low heat or in the microwave and set aside.

3 Beat the eggs and brush the bottom and sides of the dough with a little of the beaten egg. Beat the sugar, corn syrup, and vanilla extract into the beaten eggs. Add the pecans, then beat in the chocolate mixture.

4 Pour the filling into the piecrust and arrange the remaining pecan halves in concentric circles over the top. Bake in the preheated oven for 45–55 minutes, or until the filling is well risen and just set. If the edge begins to brown too quickly, cover with strips of kitchen foil. Remove from the oven and serve with ice cream.

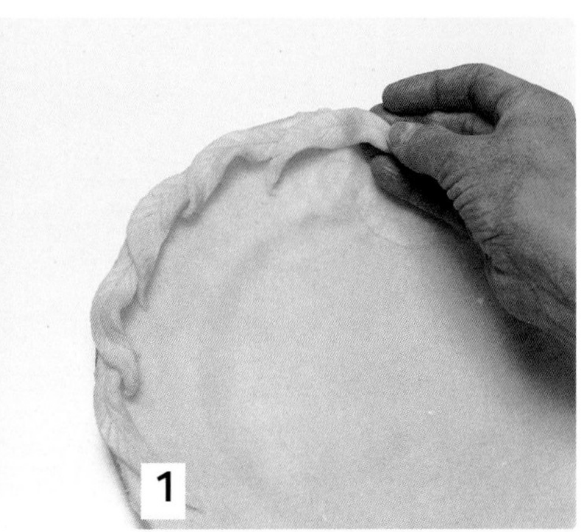
1

3

4

Pear & Chocolate Custard Tart

INGREDIENTS

Cuts into 6–8 slices

For the chocolate pie crust:

- 1 stick/¼ lb unsalted butter, softened
- ⅓ cup/2½ oz superfine sugar
- 2 tsp vanilla extract
- 1½ cups/6 oz all-purpose flour, sifted
- ⅓ cup/1½ oz unsweetened cocoa
- whipped cream, to serve

For the filling:

- 4 squares/¼ lb unsweetened chocolate, chopped
- 1 cup/8 fl oz heavy cream
- ¼ cup/2 oz superfine sugar
- 1 extra-large egg
- 1 extra-large egg yolk
- 1 tbsp crème de cacao
- 3 ripe pears

HELPFUL HINT

The chocolate dough is very soft so rolling it between sheets of plastic wrap will make it much easier to handle without having to add a lot of extra flour.

1 Preheat the oven to 375°F, 10 minutes before baking. To make the pie crust, put the butter, sugar, and vanilla extract into a food processor and blend until creamy. Add the flour and unsweetened cocoa, and process until a soft dough forms. Remove the dough, wrap in plastic wrap, and chill in the refrigerator for at least 1 hour.

2 Roll out the dough between 2 sheets of plastic wrap to an 11-inch circle. Peel off the top sheet of plastic wrap and invert the dough into a lightly greased 9-inch springform flan pan, easing the dough into the bottom and sides. Prick the bottom with a fork, then chill in the refrigerator for 1 hour.

3 Place a sheet of nonstick baking parchment and baking beans in the crust and bake blind in the preheated oven for 10 minutes. Remove the parchment and beans, and bake for a further 5 minutes. Remove and cool.

4 To make the filling, heat the chocolate, cream, and half the sugar in a medium saucepan over a low heat, stirring until melted and smooth. Remove from the heat and cool slightly before beating in the egg, egg yolk, and crème de cacao. Spread over the bottom of the pie crust.

5 Peel the pears, then cut each pear in half and carefully remove the core. Cut each half crossways into thin slices and arrange over the custard, gently fanning the slices towards the center and pressing into the chocolate custard sauce. Bake in the oven for 10 minutes.

6 Reduce the oven temperature to 350°F and sprinkle the surface evenly with the remaining sugar. Bake in the oven for 20–25 minutes, or until the custard is set and the pears are tender and glazed. Remove from the oven and leave to cool slightly. Cut into slices, then serve with spoonfuls of whipped cream.

1

2

5

Double Chocolate Banoffee Tart

INGREDIENTS

Cuts into 8 slices

2 x 14-oz cans sweetened condensed milk
6 squares/6 oz unsweetened chocolate, chopped
2 cups/1 pint whipping cream
1 tbsp corn syrup
1/4 stick/1 oz butter, diced
5 squares/5 oz white chocolate, grated or finely chopped
1 tsp vanilla extract
2–3 ripe bananas
unsweetened cocoa, for dusting

For the ginger crumb crust:

24–26 gingernut cookies, roughly crushed
1 stick/3 1/2 oz butter, melted
1/2 tbsp sugar, or to taste
1/2 tsp ground ginger

TASTY TIP

Do not assemble the tart more than 2–3 hours before serving as it will go too soft.

1 Preheat the oven to 375°F, 10 minutes before baking. Place the condensed milk in a heavy-based saucepan and place over a gentle heat. Bring to a boil, stirring constantly. Boil gently for about 3–5 minutes or until golden. Remove from the heat and let cool.

2 To make the crust, place the cookies with the melted butter, sugar, and ginger in a food processor and blend together. Press into the sides and bottom of a 9-inch loose-based flan pan with the back of a spoon. Chill in the refrigerator for 15–20 minutes, then bake in the preheated oven for 5–6 minutes. Remove from the oven and let cool.

3 Melt the unsweetened chocolate in a medium-sized saucepan with 1/2 cup/1/4 pint of the whipping cream, the corn syrup, and the butter over a low heat. Stir until smooth. Carefully pour into the crumb crust, tilting the pan to distribute the chocolate layer evenly. Chill in the refrigerator for at least 1 hour or until set.

4 Heat 1/2 cup/1/4 pint of the remaining cream until hot, then add all the white chocolate and stir until melted and smooth. Stir in the vanilla extract and strain into a bowl. Leave to cool to room temperature.

5 Scrape the cooked condensed milk into a bowl and whisk until smooth, adding a little of the remaining cream if too thick. Spread over the chocolate layer, then slice the bananas and arrange evenly over the top.

6 Whisk the remaining cream until soft peaks form. Stir a spoonful of the cream into the white chocolate mixture, then fold in the remaining cream. Spread over the bananas, swirling to the edge. Dust with unsweetened cocoa and chill in the refrigerator until ready to serve.

Chocolate Apricot Linzer Torte

INGREDIENTS

Cuts into 10–12 slices

For the chocolate almond pie crust:

3/4 cup/3 oz whole almonds, blanched
1/2 cup/1/4 lb superfine sugar
1 3/4 cups/7 1/2 oz all-purpose flour
2 tbsp unsweetened cocoa
1 tsp ground cinnamon
1/2 tsp salt
1 tbsp of grated zest of 1 orange
2 sticks/1/2 lb unsalted butter, diced
2–3 tbsp iced water

For the filling:

1 cup/3/4 lb apricot jelly
3 squares/3 oz semisweet chocolate, chopped
confectioners' sugar, for dusting

1 Preheat the oven to 190°F, 10 minutes before baking. Lightly grease an 11-inch flan pan. Place the almonds and half the sugar into a food processor and blend until finely ground. Add the remaining sugar, flour, unsweetened cocoa, cinnamon, salt, and orange zest and blend again. Add the diced butter and blend in short bursts to form coarse crumbs. Add the water 1 tablespoon at a time until the mixture starts to come together.

2 Turn onto a lightly floured surface and knead lightly, roll out, then using your fingertips, press half the dough onto the bottom and sides of the pan. Prick the bottom with a fork and chill in the refrigerator. Roll out the remaining dough between 2 pieces of plastic wrap to an 11–12 inch circle. Slide the dough onto a cookie sheet and chill in the refrigerator for 30 minutes.

3 For the filling, spread the apricot jelly evenly over the chilled pie bottom and sprinkle with the chopped chocolate.

4 Slide the dough onto a lightly floured surface and peel off the top layer of plastic wrap. Using a straight edge, cut the circle into 1/2 inch strips; let soften until slightly flexible. Place half the strips, about 1/2 inch apart, to create a lattice pattern. Press down on each side of each crossing to accentuate the effect. Press the ends of the strips to the edge, cutting off any excess. Bake in the preheated oven for 35 minutes, or until cooked. Let cool before dusting with confectioners' sugar and serve cut into slices.

TASTY TIP

When making the dough do not allow it to form into a ball or it will be tough.

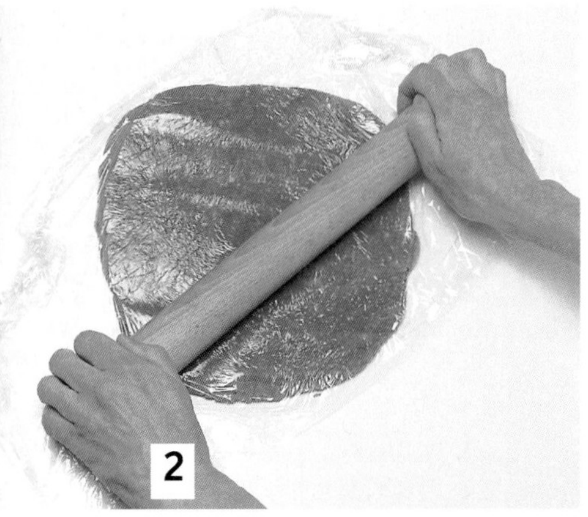
2

3

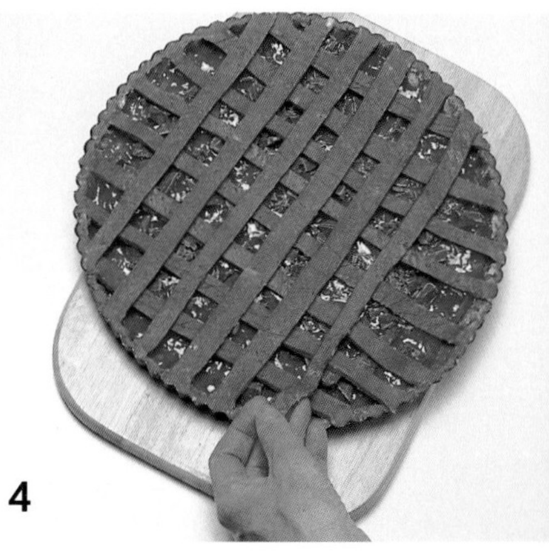
4

Chocolate Peanut Butter Pie

INGREDIENTS

Cuts into 8 slices

22–24 chocolate wafers or peanut butter cookies
1 stick/3½ oz butter, melted
1–2 tbsp sugar
1 tsp vanilla extract
1½ tbsp gelatin
½ cup/3½ oz superfine sugar
1 tbsp cornstarch
½ tsp salt
1 cup/8 fl oz milk
2 extra-large eggs, separated
2 extra-large egg yolks
3½ squares/3½ oz unsweetened chocolate, chopped
2 tbsp rum or 2 tsp vanilla extract
½ cup/¼ lb smooth peanut butter
1 cup/½ pint heavy cream
chocolate curls, to decorate

1 Place the wafers or cookies with the melted butter, sugar, and vanilla extract in a food processor and blend together. Press into the bottom of a 9-inch flan pan. Chill in the refrigerator for 15–20 minutes.

2 Place 3 tablespoons cold water in a bowl and sprinkle over the powdered gelatin, leave until softened.

3 Blend half the sugar with the cornstarch and salt in a heavy-based saucepan and gradually beat in the milk. Bring to a boil, then reduce the heat and boil gently for 1–2 minutes, or until thickened and smooth, stirring constantly.

4 Beat all the egg yolks together, then beat in half the hot milk mixture until blended. Beat in the remaining milk mixture, return to a clean saucepan, and cook gently until the mixture comes to a boil and thickens. Boil, stirring vigorously, for 1 minute, then pour a quarter of the custard into a bowl. Add the chopped chocolate and rum or vanilla extract and stir until the chocolate has melted and the mixture is smooth. Pour into the chocolate crust and chill in the refrigerator until set.

5 Beat the softened gelatin into the remaining custard and beat until thoroughly dissolved. Beat in the peanut butter until melted and smooth. Beat the egg whites until stiff, then beat in the remaining sugar, 1 tablespoon at a time.

6 Whip the cream until soft peaks form. Fold ½ cup/4 fl oz of the cream into the custard, then fold in the egg whites. Spread the peanut butter cream mixture over the chocolate layer. Spread or pipe over the surface with the remaining cream, forming decorative swirls. Decorate with chocolate curls and chill in the refrigerator until ready to serve.

1

3

4

Mini Pistachio & Chocolate Strudels

INGREDIENTS

Makes 24

5 large sheets phyllo pastry dough
½ stick/2 oz butter, melted
1–2 tbsp superfine sugar, for sprinkling
2 squares/2 oz white chocolate, melted, to decorate

For the filling:

1 cup/¼ lb unsalted pistachios, finely chopped
3 tbsp superfine sugar
2 squares/2 oz unsweetened chocolate, finely chopped
1–2 tsp rosewater
1 tbsp confectioners' sugar, for dusting

1 Preheat the oven to 325°F, 10 minutes before baking. Lightly grease 2 large cookie sheets. For the filling, mix the finely chopped pistachio nuts, the sugar, and unsweetened chocolate in a bowl. Sprinkle with the rosewater, stir lightly together, and set aside.

2 Cut each phyllo sheet into 4 to make 9 x 7-inch rectangles. Place 1 rectangle on the work surface and brush with a little melted butter. Place another rectangle on top and brush with a little more butter. Sprinkle with a little superfine sugar and spread about 1 spoonful of the filling along one short end. Fold the short end over the filling, then fold in the long edges and roll up. Place on the cookie sheet seam-side down. Continue with the remaining dough sheets and filling until both are used.

3 Brush each strudel with the remaining melted butter and sprinkle with a little superfine sugar. Bake in the preheated oven for 20 minutes, or until golden brown and the crust is crisp.

4 Remove from the oven and leave on the cookie sheet for 2 minutes, then transfer to a wire rack. Dust with confectioners' sugar. Place the melted white chocolate in a small piping bag fitted with a plain writing tip and pipe squiggles over the strudel. Leave to set before serving.

TASTY TIP

Keep the unused phyllo dough covered with a clean damp dish towel to prevent it from drying out.

1

2

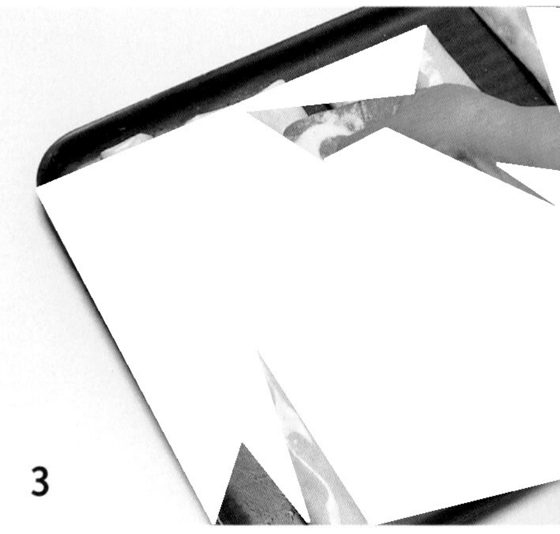
3

Raspberry Chocolate Ganache & Berry Tartlets

INGREDIENTS

Serves 8

1 quantity chocolate pie crust (see page 144)
2 cups/1 pint heavy cream
3/4 cup/10 oz seedless raspberry jelly
8 squares/1/2 lb unsweetened chocolate, chopped
6 1/2 cups/1 1/2 lb raspberries or other summer berries
1/4 cup/2 fl oz framboise liqueur
1 tbsp superfine sugar
sour cream, to serve

1 Preheat the oven to 400°F, 15 minutes before cooking. Make the pie crust and use to line 8 3-inch tartlet pans. Bake blind in the preheated oven for 12 minutes.

2 Place 3/4 cup/14 fl oz of the cream and half of the raspberry jelly in a saucepan and bring to a boil, beating constantly to dissolve the jelly. Remove from the heat and add the chocolate all at once, stirring until the chocolate has melted.

3 Pour into the dough-lined tartlet pans, shaking gently to distribute the ganache evenly. Chill in the refrigerator for 1 hour or until set.

4 Place the berries in a large, shallow bowl. Heat the remaining raspberry jelly with half the framboise liqueur over a medium heat until melted and bubbling. Drizzle over the berries and toss gently to coat.

5 Divide the berries among the tartlets, piling them up if necessary. Chill in the refrigerator until ready to serve.

6 Remove the tartlets from the refrigerator for at least 30 minutes before serving. Using an electric mixer, beat the remaining cream with the superfine sugar and the remaining framboise liqueur until it is thick and softly peaking. Serve with the tartlets and sour cream.

TASTY TIP

Try substituting an equal quantity of white chocolate for the unsweetened chocolate in this recipe, as raspberries go very well with it.

1

2

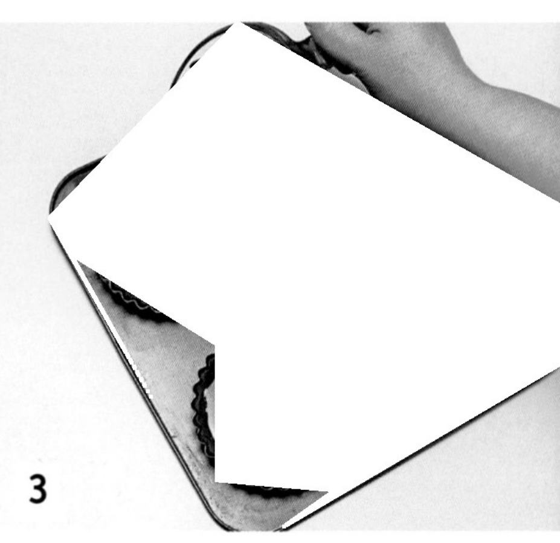
3

Chocolaty Puffs

INGREDIENTS

Makes 12 large puffs

For the choux pastry:

- $1\frac{1}{4}$ cups/5 oz all-purpose flour
- 2 tbsp unsweetened cocoa
- $\frac{1}{2}$ tsp salt
- 1 tbsp superfine sugar
- 1 stick/$\frac{1}{4}$ lb butter, cut into pieces
- 5 extra-large eggs

For the chocolate cream filling:

- 8 squares/$\frac{1}{2}$ lb unsweetened chocolate, chopped
- 2 cups/1 pint heavy cream
- 1 tbsp superfine sugar (optional)
- 2 tbsp crème de cacao (optional)

For the chocolate sauce:

- 8 squares/$\frac{1}{2}$ lb unsweetened chocolate
- 1 cup/$\frac{1}{2}$ pint heavy cream
- $\frac{1}{2}$ cup/2 oz butter, diced
- 1–2 tbsp corn syrup
- 1 tsp vanilla extract

1 Preheat the oven to 425°F, 15 minutes before baking. Lightly grease a large cookie sheet. To make the choux pastry dough, sift the flour and unsweetened cocoa together. Place 1 cup/9 fl oz of water, the salt, sugar, and butter in a saucepan and bring to a boil. Remove from the heat and add the flour mixture all at once, beating vigorously with a wooden spoon until the mixture forms a ball in the center of the saucepan. Return to the heat and cook for 1 minute stirring, then cool slightly.

2 Using an electric mixer, beat in 4 of the eggs, 1 at a time, beating well after each addition. Beat the last egg and add a little at a time until the dough is thick and shiny and just falls from a spoon when tapped lightly on the side of the saucepan.

3 Pipe or spoon 12 large puffs onto the prepared cookie sheet, leaving space between them. Cook in the preheated oven for 30–35 minutes, or until puffy and golden. Remove from the oven, slice off the top third of each bun, and return to the oven for 5 minutes to dry out. Remove and let cool.

4 For the filling, heat the chocolate with $\frac{1}{2}$ cup/4 fl oz of the heavy cream and 1 tablespoon of superfine sugar, if using, stirring until smooth, then leave to cool. Whisk the remaining cream until soft peaks form and stir in the crème de cacao, if using. Quickly fold the cream into the chocolate, then spoon or pipe into the choux buns and place the lids on top.

5 Place all the ingredients for the sauce in a small saucepan and heat gently, stirring until smooth. Remove from the heat and let cool, stirring occasionally until thickened. Pour over the puffs and serve immediately.

1

3

5

Rice Pudding & Chocolate Tart

INGREDIENTS

Serves 8

1 quantity chocolate pie crust (see page 144)
1 tsp unsweetened cocoa, for dusting

For the chocolate ganache:

1 cup/7 fl oz heavy cream
1 tbsp corn syrup
6 squares/6 oz unsweetened chocolate, chopped
1 tbsp butter
1 tsp vanilla extract

For the rice pudding:

4 cups/1¾ pints milk
½ tsp salt
1 vanilla pod
½ cup/3½ oz long-grain white rice
1 tbsp cornstarch
2 tbsp sugar

To decorate:

few fresh blueberries
sprigs fresh mint

1 Preheat the oven to 400°F, 15 minutes before baking. Roll the chocolate dough out and use to line a 9-inch flan pan. Place a sheet of nonstick baking parchment and baking beans in the pan and bake blind in the preheated oven for 15 minutes.

2 For the ganache, place the cream and corn syrup in a heavy-based saucepan and bring to a boil. Remove from the heat and add the chocolate all at once, stirring until smooth. Beat in the butter and vanilla extract, pour into the baked pie crust, and set aside.

3 For the rice pudding, bring the milk and salt to a boil in a medium-sized saucepan. Split the vanilla pod and scrape the seeds into the milk and add the vanilla pod. Sprinkle in the rice, then bring to a boil. Reduce the heat and simmer until the rice is tender and the milk is creamy. Remove from the heat.

4 Blend the cornstarch and sugar together, then stir in 2 tablespoons water to make a paste. Stir a little of the hot rice mixture into the cornstarch mixture, then stir the cornstarch mixture into the rice. Bring to a boil and cook, stirring constantly until thickened. Set the bottom of the saucepan into a bowl of iced water and stir until cooled and thickened. Spoon the rice pudding into the tart, smoothing the surface. Let set. Dust with unsweetened cocoa, decorate with a few blueberries and fresh mint to serve.

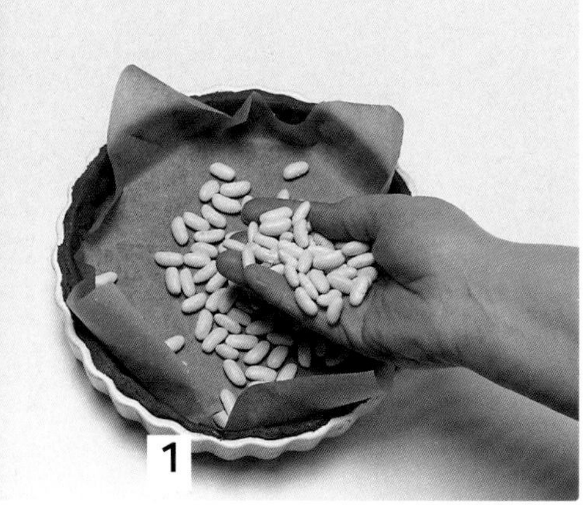
1

2

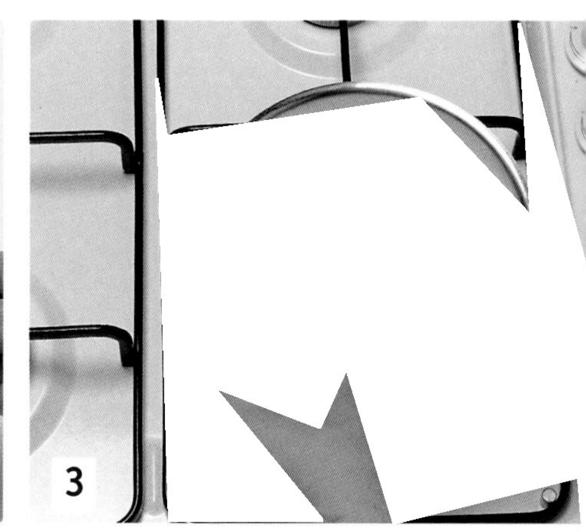
3

Chocolate Lemon Tartlets

INGREDIENTS

Makes 10

1 quantity sweet pie crust dough (see page 140)
3/4 cup/6 fl oz heavy cream
6 squares/6 oz unsweetened chocolate, chopped
1/4 stick/2 tbsp butter, diced
1 tsp vanilla extract
1 cup/3/4 lb lemon curd
1 cup/8 fl oz prepared custard sauce
1 cup/8 fl oz light cream
1/2 –1 tsp almond extract

To decorate:

grated chocolate
slivered almonds, toasted

TASTY TIP

Lemon curd is very easy to make. In a medium-sized heatproof bowl, mix together 3/4 cup/6 oz of superfine sugar, the grated rind, and juice of 2 large lemons and 4 extra-large eggs. Add 2/3 cup/1/4 lb cubed unsalted butter and place the bowl over a saucepan of gently simmering water. Stir often until thickened, about 20 minutes. Let cool and use as above.

1 Preheat the oven to 400°F, 15 minutes before baking. Roll the prepared dough out on a lightly floured surface and use to line 10 x 3-inch tartlet pans. Place a small piece of crumpled kitchen foil in each and bake blind in the preheated oven for 12 minutes. Remove from the oven and let cool.

2 Bring the cream to a boil, then remove from the heat and add the chocolate all at once. Stir until smooth and melted. Beat in the butter and vanilla extract, pour into the tartlets, and leave to cool.

3 Beat the lemon curd until soft and spoon a thick layer over the chocolate in each tartlet, spreading gently to the edges. Do not chill in the refrigerator or the chocolate will be too firm.

4 Place the prepared custard sauce into a large bowl and gradually beat in the cream and almond extract until the custard sauce is smooth and runny.

5 To serve, spoon a little custard sauce onto a plate and place a tartlet in the center. Sprinkle with grated chocolate and almonds, then serve.

1

2

3

Fudgy Mocha Pie with Espresso Custard Sauce

INGREDIENTS

Cuts into 10 slices

4 squares/¼ lb unsweetened chocolate, chopped
1 stick/¼ lb butter, diced
1 tbsp instant espresso powder
4 extra-large eggs
1 tbsp corn syrup
½ cup/¼ lb superfine sugar
1 tsp ground cinnamon
3 tbsp milk
confectioners' sugar, for dusting
few fresh strawberries, to serve

For the espresso custard sauce:

2–3 tbsp instant espresso powder, or to taste
1 cup/8 fl oz prepared custard sauce
1 cup/8 fl oz light cream
2 tbsp coffee-flavored liqueur (optional)

1 Preheat the oven to 350°F, 10 minutes before serving. Line with kitchen foil or lightly grease a 9-inch, deep pie plate. Melt the chocolate and butter in a small saucepan over a low heat and stir until smooth, then set aside. Dissolve the instant espresso powder in 1–2 tablespoons hot water and set aside.

2 Beat the eggs with the corn syrup, sugar, dissolved espresso powder, cinnamon, and milk until blended. Add the melted chocolate mixture and beat until blended. Pour into the pie plate.

3 Bake the pie in the preheated oven for about 20–25 minutes, or until the edge has set but the center is still very soft. Let cool, remove from the plate, then dust lightly with confectioners' sugar.

4 To make the custard sauce, dissolve the instant espresso powder with 2–3 tablespoons hot water, then beat into the prepared custard sauce. Slowly add the light cream, beating constantly, then stir in the coffee-flavored liqueur, if using. Serve slices of the pie in a pool of espresso custard with strawberries.

1

2

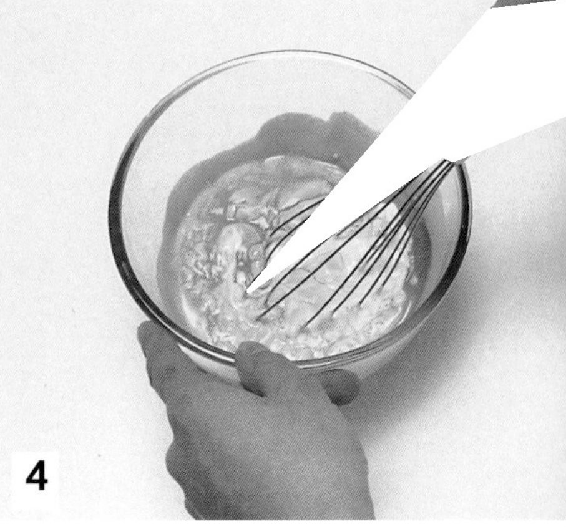
4

Frozen Mississippi Mud Pie

INGREDIENTS

Cuts 6–8 slices

1 quantity ginger crumb crust (see page 146)
2 cups/1 pint chocolate ice cream
2 cups/1 pint coffee-flavored ice cream

For the chocolate topping:

6 squares/6 oz unsweetened chocolate, chopped
1/4 cup/2 fl oz light cream
1 tbsp corn syrup
1 tsp vanilla extract
2 squares/2 oz white and semisweet chocolate, coarsely grated

HELPFUL HINT

Use the best-quality ice cream that is available for this recipe. Look for chocolate ice cream with added ingredients such as chocolate chips, pieces of toffee, or rippled chocolate. If preferred you can add some raspberries, chopped nuts, or small pieces of chopped white chocolate to both the chocolate and coffee ice cream.

1 Prepare the crumb crust and use to line a 9-inch loose-based cake pan and freeze for 30 minutes.

2 Soften the ice creams at room temperature for about 25 minutes. Spoon the chocolate ice cream into the crumb crust, spreading it evenly over the bottom, then spoon the coffee ice cream over the chocolate ice cream, mounding it slightly in the center. Return to the freezer to refreeze the ice cream.

3 For the topping, heat the unsweetened chocolate with the cream, corn syrup, and vanilla extract in a saucepan. Stir until the chocolate has melted and is smooth. Pour into a bowl and chill in the refrigerator, stirring occasionally, until cold but not set.

4 Spread the cooled chocolate mixture over the top of the frozen pie. Sprinkle with the grated chocolate and return to the freezer for 1 1/2 hours or until firm. Serve at room temperature.

1

2

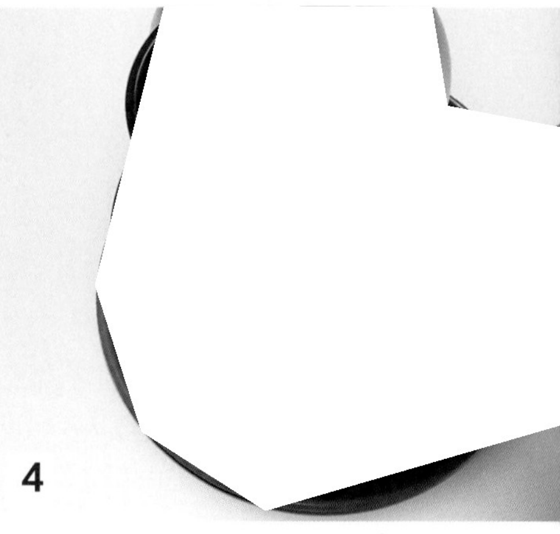
4

White Chocolate Mousse & Strawberry Tart

INGREDIENTS

Cuts into 10 slices

1 quantity sweet pie crust dough (see page 140)
1/4 cup/2 1/2 oz strawberry jelly
1/2 tbsp kirsch or framboise liqueur
4–6 cups/1–1 1/2 lb ripe strawberries, sliced lengthways

For the white chocolate mousse:

9 squares/9 oz white chocolate, chopped
1 1/2 cups/3/4 lb heavy cream
3 tbsp kirsch or framboise liqueur
1–2 extra-large egg whites (optional)

HELPFUL HINT

This recipe contains raw egg whites, which should be eaten with caution by vulnerable groups including the elderly, the young, and pregnant women. If you are worried, omit them from the recipe.

1 Preheat the oven to 400°F, 15 minutes before baking. Roll the prepared dough out on a lightly floured surface and use to line a 10-inch flan pan.

2 Line with either kitchen foil or nonstick baking parchment and baking beans then bake blind in the preheated oven for 15–20 minutes. Remove the foil or baking parchment and return to the oven for a further 5 minutes.

3 To make the mousse, place the white chocolate with 2 tablespoons water and 1/2 cup/4 fl oz of the cream in a saucepan and heat gently, stirring until the chocolate has melted and is smooth. Remove from the heat, stir in the kirsch or framboise liqueur and cool.

4 Whip the remaining cream until soft peaks form. Fold a spoonful of the cream into the cooled white chocolate mixture, then fold in the remaining cream. If using, beat the egg whites until stiff and gently fold into the white-chocolate cream mixture to make a softer, lighter mousse. Chill in the refrigerator for 15–20 minutes.

5 Heat the strawberry jelly with the kirsch or framboise liqueur and brush or spread half the mixture onto the bottom of the pie crust. Leave to cool.

6 Spread the chilled chocolate mousse over the jelly and arrange the sliced strawberries in concentric circles over the mousse. If necessary, reheat the strawberry jelly and glaze the strawberries lightly.

7 Chill the tart in the refrigerator for about 3–4 hours, or until the chocolate mousse has set. Cut into slices and serve.

3

4

6

Chocolate Raspberry Pastries

INGREDIENTS

Serves 6

1 lb puff pastry dough, thawed if frozen
1 quantity chocolate raspberry ganache (see page 154), chilled
6 cups/1½ lbs fresh raspberries, plus extra for decorating
confectioners' sugar, for dusting

For the raspberry sauce:

2 cups/½ lb fresh raspberries
2 tbsp seedless raspberry jelly
1–2 tbsp superfine sugar, or to taste
2 tbsp lemon juice or framboise liqueur

HELPFUL HINT

If you prefer, make 1 big pastry by leaving the 3 strips whole in step 2. Slice the finished pastry with a sharp serrated knife.

1 Preheat the oven to 400°F, 15 minutes before baking. Lightly grease a large cookie sheet and sprinkle with a little water. Roll out the puff pastry dough on a lightly floured surface to a rectangle about 17 x 11 inches. Cut into 3 long strips. Mark each strip crossways at 2½-inch intervals using a sharp knife; this will make cutting the baked puff pastry easier and neater. Carefully transfer to the cookie sheet, keeping the edges as straight as possible.

2 Bake in the preheated oven for 20 minutes or until well risen and golden brown. Place on a wire rack and let cool. Carefully transfer each rectangle to a work surface, and using a sharp knife, trim the long edges straight. Cut along the knife marks to make 18 rectangles.

3 Place all the ingredients for the raspberry sauce in a food processor and blend until smooth. If the puree is too thick, add a little water. Taste and adjust the sweetness if necessary. Strain into a bowl, cover, and chill in the refrigerator.

4 Place 1 pastry rectangle on the work surface flat-side down, spread with a little chocolate ganache, and sprinkle with a few fresh raspberries. Spread a second rectangle with a little ganache, place over the first, pressing gently, then sprinkle with a few raspberries. Place a third rectangle on top, flat-side up, and spread with a little chocolate ganache.

5 Arrange some raspberries on top and dust lightly with a little confectioners' sugar. Repeat with the remaining dough rectangles, chocolate ganache, and fresh raspberries.

6 Chill in the refrigerator until required and serve with the raspberry sauce and any remaining fresh raspberries.

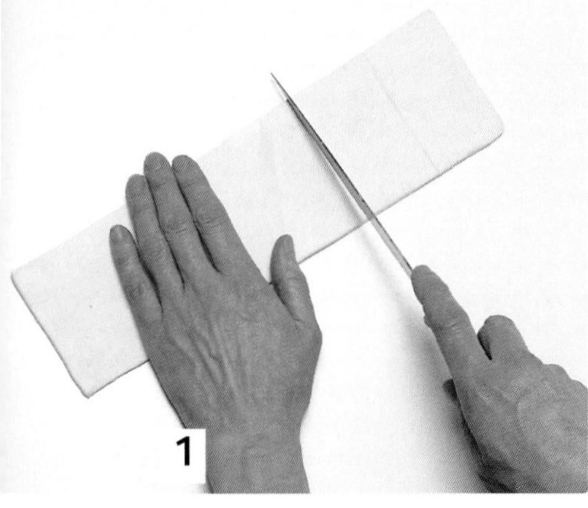
1

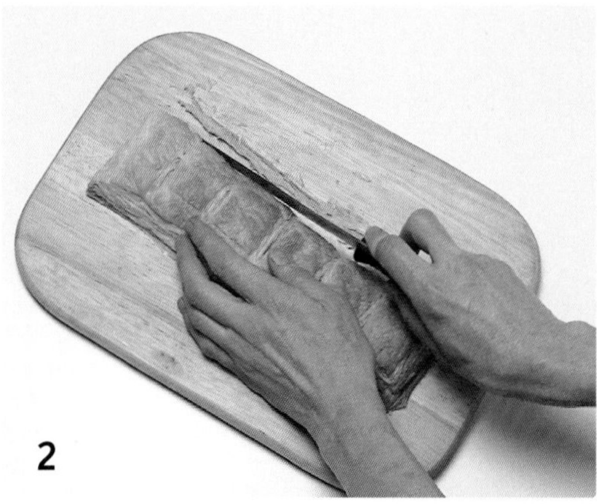
2

4

Chocolate Brioche Bake

INGREDIENTS

Serves 6

7 squares/7 oz unsweetened chocolate, broken into pieces
3/4 stick/3 oz unsalted butter
1 large/1/2 lb brioche, sliced
1 tsp pure orange oil or 1 tbsp grated orange rind
1/2 tsp nutmeg, freshly grated
3 eggs, beaten
2 tbsp/1 oz unrefined superfine sugar
2 1/2 cups/1 pint milk
unsweetened cocoa and confectioners' sugar, for dusting

1 Preheat the oven to 350°F, 10 minutes before baking. Lightly grease or butter a 1 3/4-quart/3-pint ovenproof dish. Melt the chocolate with 2 tbsp/1 oz of the butter in a heatproof bowl set over a saucepan of simmering water. Stir until smooth.

2 Arrange half of the sliced brioche in the ovenproof dish, overlapping the slices slightly, then pour over half of the melted chocolate. Repeat the layers, finishing with a layer of chocolate.

3 Melt the remaining butter in a saucepan. Remove from the heat and stir in the orange oil or rind, the nutmeg, and the beaten eggs. Continuing to stir, add the sugar and finally the milk. Beat thoroughly and pour over the brioche. Leave to stand for 30 minutes before baking.

4 Bake on the center shelf in the preheated oven for 45 minutes, or until the custard is set and the topping is golden brown. Leave to stand for 5 minutes, then dust with unsweetened cocoa and confectioners' sugar. Serve warm.

HELPFUL HINT

Croissants, fruit buns, or fruit loaves are also suitable for this recipe. It is important that the dish is left to stand for 30 minutes before baking—do not be tempted to omit this step.

1

2

3

Mocha Pie

INGREDIENTS

Serves 4–6

1 x 9-inch ready-made sweet pie shell

For the filling:

4 squares/¼ lb unsweetened chocolate, broken into pieces
1½ sticks/6 oz unsalted butter
1 cup/½ lb soft brown sugar
1 tsp vanilla extract
3 tbsp strong black coffee

For the topping:

2 cups/1 pint heavy cream
½ cup/2 oz confectioners' sugar
2 tsp vanilla extract
1 tsp instant coffee dissolved in 1 tsp boiling water, cooled
unsweetened and white chocolate, grated, to decorate

1. Place the prepared pie shell on a large serving plate and set aside. Melt the chocolate in a heatproof bowl set over a saucepan of simmering water. Make sure the water is not touching the bottom of the bowl. Remove from the heat, stir until smooth, and leave to cool.

2. Cream the butter, soft brown sugar, and vanilla extract until light and fluffy, then beat in the cooled chocolate. Add the strong black coffee, pour into the pie shell, and chill in the refrigerator for about 30 minutes.

3. For the topping, whisk the cream until beginning to thicken, then beat in the sugar and vanilla extract. Continue to whisk until the cream is softly peaking. Spoon just under half of the cream into a separate bowl and fold in the dissolved coffee.

4. Spread the remaining cream over the filling in the pie shell. Spoon the coffee-flavored whipped cream evenly over the top, then swirl it decoratively with a palate knife. Sprinkle with grated chocolate and chill in the refrigerator until ready to serve.

HELPFUL HINT

Using a ready-made pie shell makes this a quickly made store-cupboard pie that looks very impressive.

2

3

4

Crunchy Rhubarb Crisp

INGREDIENTS

Serves 6

1 cup/¼ lb all-purpose flour
½ stick/2 oz softened butter
⅔ cup/2 oz rolled oats
¼ cup/2 oz light brown sugar
1 tbsp sesame seeds
½ tsp ground cinnamon
1 lb fresh rhubarb (about 4 large stalks)
¼ cup/2 oz superfine sugar
custard or cream, to serve

TASTY TIP

To make homemade custard, pour 2½ cups/1 pint of milk with a few drops of vanilla extract into a saucepan and bring to a boil. Remove from the heat and let cool. Meanwhile, beat 5 egg yolks and 3 tablespoons superfine sugar together in a mixing bowl until thick and pale in color. Add the milk, stir, and strain into a heavy-based saucepan. Cook the custard on a low heat, stirring constantly until the consistency of heavy cream. Pour over the rhubarb crisp and serve.

1 Preheat the oven to 350°F. Place the flour in a large bowl and cut the butter into cubes. Add to the flour and rub in with the fingertips until the mixture looks like fine breadcrumbs, or blend for a few seconds in a food processor.

2 Stir in the rolled oats, light brown sugar, sesame seeds, and cinnamon. Mix well and set aside.

3 Prepare the rhubarb by removing the thick ends of the stalks and cut diagonally into 1-inch chunks. Wash thoroughly and pat dry with a clean dishtowel. Place the rhubarb in a 1¼-quart/2-pint pie dish.

4 Sprinkle the superfine sugar over the rhubarb and top with the crisp mixture. Level the top of the crisp so that all the fruit is well covered and press down firmly. If liked, sprinkle the top with a little extra superfine sugar.

5 Place on a cookie sheet and bake in the preheated oven for 40–50 minutes, or until the fruit is soft and the topping is golden brown. Sprinkle the dessert with some more superfine sugar and serve hot with custard sauce or cream.

2

3

4

Chocolate Crepes

INGREDIENTS

Makes approx. 8

For the crepes:

$^2/_3$ cup/3 oz all-purpose flour
1 tbsp unsweetened cocoa
1 tsp superfine sugar
$^1/_2$ tsp nutmeg, freshly grated
2 eggs
$^3/_4$ cup/6 fl oz milk
$^3/_4$ stick/3 oz unsalted butter, melted

For the mango sauce:

1 ripe mango, peeled and diced
$^1/_4$ cup/2 fl oz white wine
2 tbsp superfine sugar
2 tbsp rum

For the filling:

8 squares/$^1/_2$ lb unsweetened chocolate
$^1/_3$ cup/3 fl oz heavy cream
3 eggs, separated
2 tbsp/1 oz unrefined superfine sugar

1 Preheat the oven to 400°F, 15 minutes before cooking. To make the crepes, sift the flour, unsweetened cocoa, sugar, and nutmeg into a bowl and make a well in the center. Beat the eggs and milk together, then gradually beat into the flour mixture to form a batter. Stir in $^1/_4$ cup/2 oz of the melted butter and leave to stand for 1 hour.

2 Heat a 7-inch nonstick skillet pan and brush with a little melted butter. Add about 3 tablespoons of the batter and swirl to cover the bottom of the pan. Cook over a medium heat for 1–2 minutes, flip over, and cook for a further 40 seconds. Repeat with the remaining batter. Stack the crepes, interleaving with waxed paper.

3 To make the sauce, place the mango, white wine, and sugar in a saucepan and bring to a boil over a medium heat, then simmer for 2–3 minutes, stirring constantly. When the mixture has thickened add the rum. Chill in the refrigerator.

4 For the filling, melt the chocolate and cream in a small heavy-based saucepan over a medium heat. Stir until smooth, then leave to cool. Beat the egg yolks with the superfine sugar for 3–5 minutes, or until the mixture is pale and creamy, then beat in the chocolate mixture.

5 Beat the egg whites until stiff, then add a little to the chocolate mixture. Stir in the remainder. Spoon a little of the mixture onto a crepe. Fold in half, then fold in half again, forming a triangle. Repeat with the remaining crepes.

6 Brush the crepes with a little melted butter and bake in the preheated oven for 15–20 minutes or until the filling is set. Serve hot or cold with the mango sauce.

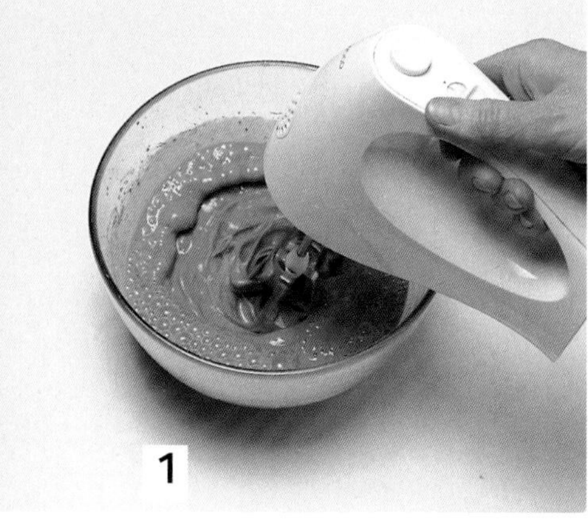
1

2

5

Iced Bakewell Tart

INGREDIENTS

Cuts into 10 slices

For the dough:
1 1/2 cups/6 oz all-purpose flour
pinch salt
5 tbsp/2 1/2 oz butter, cut into small pieces
4 tbsp/2 oz shortening, cut into small pieces
2 medium egg yolks, beaten

For the filling:
1 stick plus 1 tbsp/1/4 lb butter, melted
2/3 cup/1/4 lb superfine sugar
1 cup/1/4 lb almonds, ground
2 extra-large eggs, beaten
few drops of almond extract
2 tbsp seedless raspberry jelly

For the frosting:
1 cup/1/4 lb confectioners' sugar, sifted
6–8 tsp fresh lemon juice
1/4 cup/1 oz slivered almonds, toasted

TASTY TIP
It is not essential to use raspberry jelly. Use any seedless jelly available. Blackcurrant jelly would work particularly well.

1 Preheat the oven to 400°F. Place the flour and salt in a bowl, rub in the butter and shortening until the mixture resembles bread crumbs. Alternatively, blend quickly, in short bursts in a food processor.

2 Add the eggs with sufficient water to make a soft, pliable dough. Knead lightly on a floured board then chill in the refrigerator for about 30 minutes. Roll out the dough and use to line a 9-inch loose-bottomed flan pan.

3 For the filling, mix together the melted butter, sugar, almonds, and beaten eggs and add a few drops of almond extract. Spread the bottom of the pie shell with the raspberry jelly and spoon over the egg mixture.

4 Bake in the preheated oven for about 30 minutes, or until the filling is firm and golden brown. Remove from the oven and let cool completely.

5 When the tart is cold, make the frosting by mixing together the confectioners' sugar and lemon juice, a little at a time, until the frosting is smooth and of a spreadable consistency.

6 Spread the frosting over the tart, leave to set for 2–3 minutes, and sprinkle with the almonds. Chill in the refrigerator for about 10 minutes and serve.

2

3

6

Apricot & Almond Slice

INGREDIENTS

Cuts into 10 slices

2 tbsp light brown sugar
1/4 cup/1 oz slivered almonds
14-oz can apricot halves, drained
1 cup/1/2 lb butter, softened
1 cup/1/2 lb superfine sugar
4 eggs
1 3/4 cups/7 oz self-rising flour
1/4 cup/1 oz almonds, ground
1/2 tsp almond extract
1/3 cup/2 oz ready-to-eat dried apricots, chopped
3 tbsp clear honey
3 tbsp almonds, roughly chopped and toasted

1 Preheat the oven to 350°F. Grease an 8-inch, square pan and line with nonstick baking parchment.

2 Sprinkle the sugar and the slivered almonds over the paper, then arrange the apricot halves cut side down on top.

3 Cream the butter and sugar together in a large bowl until light and fluffy.

4 Gradually beat the eggs into the butter mixture, adding a spoonful of flour after each addition of egg.

5 When all the eggs have been added, stir in the remaining flour and ground almonds and mix thoroughly.

6 Add the almond extract and the apricots and stir well.

7 Spoon the mixture into the prepared pan, being careful not to dislodge the apricot halves. Bake in the preheated oven for 1 hour, or until golden and firm to touch.

8 Remove from the oven and let cool slightly for 15–20 minutes. Turn out carefully, discard the lining paper, and transfer to a serving dish. Pour the honey over the top of the cake, sprinkle on the toasted almonds, and serve.

HELPFUL HINT

This cake should keep for 3–5 days if stored correctly. Let the cake cool completely, then remove from the pan, and discard the lining paper. Store in an airtight container lined with waxed paper or baking parchment and keep in a cool place.

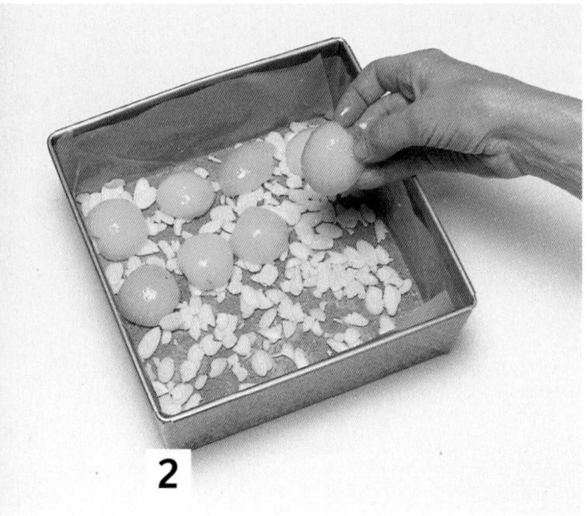
2

5

8

Strawberry Flan

INGREDIENTS

Serves 6

For the sweet pie crust:

1½ cups/6 oz all-purpose flour
4 tbsp/2 oz butter
4 tbsp/2 oz shortening
2 tsp superfine sugar
1 egg yolk, beaten

For the filling:

1 egg, plus 1 extra egg yolk
4 tbsp/2 oz superfine sugar
3 tbsp/1 oz all-purpose flour
2½ cups/½ pint milk
few drops vanilla extract
3 cups/1 lb strawberries, cleaned and hulled
leaves mint, to decorate

1 Preheat the oven to 400°F. Place the flour, butter, and shortening in a food processor and blend until the mixture resembles fine bread crumbs. Stir in the sugar, then with the machine running, add the egg yolk and enough water to make a fairly stiff dough. Knead lightly, cover, and chill in the refrigerator for 30 minutes.

2 Roll out the dough and use to line a 9-inch loose-bottomed flan pan. Place a piece of waxed paper in the pie shell and cover with baking beans or rice. Bake in the preheated oven for 15–20 minutes, until just firm. Set aside until cool.

3 Make the filling by beating the eggs and sugar together until thick and pale. Gradually stir in the flour and then the milk. Pour into a small saucepan and simmer for 3–4 minutes stirring throughout.

4 Add the vanilla extract to taste, then pour into a bowl and leave to cool. Cover with waxed paper to prevent a skin from forming.

5 When the filling is cold, beat until smooth, then pour onto the cooked pie shell. Slice the strawberries and arrange on the top of the filling. Decorate with the mint leaves and serve.

TASTY TIP

In the summer, why not try topping the flan with a variety of mixed fruits? If liked, heat 3 tablespoons seedless raspberry jelly with 2 teaspoons lemon juice. Stir until smooth, then use to brush over the fruit. Let set before serving.

2

3

5

Rich Double-crust Plum Pie

INGREDIENTS

Serves 6

For the dough:

3/4 stick/3 oz butter
1/4 cup/3 oz shortening
2 cups/1/2 lb all-purpose flour
2 egg yolks

For the filling:

1 lb fresh plums (about 6)
1/4 cup/2 oz superfine sugar
1 tbsp milk
a little extra superfine sugar

1 Preheat the oven to 400°F. Make the dough by rubbing the butter and shortening into the flour until it resembles fine bread crumbs or blend in a food processor. Add the egg yolks and enough water to make a soft dough. Knead lightly, then wrap, and leave in the refrigerator for about 30 minutes.

2 Meanwhile, prepare the fruit. Rinse and dry the plums, then cut in half and remove the pits. Slice the plums into chunks and cook in a saucepan with 2 tbsp/1 oz of the sugar and 2 tablespoons water for 5–7 minutes, or until slightly softened. Remove from the heat and add the remaining sugar to taste and let cool.

3 Roll out half the chilled dough on a lightly floured surface and use to line the bottom and sides of a 1 1/4-quart/2-pint casserole dish. Let the dough hang over the edge of the dish. Spoon in the prepared plums.

4 Roll out the remaining dough to use as the lid and brush the edge with a little water. Wrap the dough around the rolling pin and place over the plums.

5 Press the edges together to seal and mark a decorative edge of the pie around the rim of the dough by pinching with the thumb and forefinger or using the back of a fork.

6 Brush the lid with milk, and make a few slits in the top. Use any trimmings to decorate the top of the pie with dough leaves. Place on a cookie sheet and bake in the preheated oven for 30 minutes, or until golden brown. Sprinkle with a little superfine sugar and serve hot or cold.

HELPFUL HINT

Plums are seasonal, so it may be necessary to use varieties that have been imported. Alternatively, buy plums in season, then halve, store, and freeze them, then use as required.

2

4

5

Baked Apple Dumplings

INGREDIENTS

Serves 4

2 cups/$^1/_2$ lb self-rising flour
$^1/_4$ tsp salt
$^1/_2$ cup/$^1/_4$ lb shredded suet
4 cooking apples
4–6 tsp mince pie filling
1 egg white, beaten
2 tsp superfine sugar
custard sauce or vanilla sauce, to serve

TASTY TIP

To make vanilla sauce, blend 1$^1/_2$ tablespoons cornstarch with 3 tablespoons milk to a smooth paste. Bring just under 1$^1/_4$ cups/ $^1/_2$ pint milk to just below boiling point. Stir in the cornstarch paste and cook over a gentle heat, stirring throughout until thickened and smooth. Remove from the heat and add 1 tablespoon superfine sugar, a knob of butter and $^1/_2$ teaspoon vanilla extract. Stir until the sugar and butter have melted, then serve.

1 Preheat the oven to 400°F. Lightly grease a cookie sheet. Place the flour and salt in a bowl and stir in the suet.

2 Add just enough water to the mixture to mix to a soft but not sticky dough, using the fingertips.

3 Turn the dough onto a lightly floured board and knead lightly into a ball.

4 Divide the dough into 4 pieces and roll out each piece into a thin square, large enough to encase the apples.

5 Peel and core the apples and place 1 apple in the center of each square of dough.

6 Fill the center of the apple with mince pie filling, brush the edges of each dough square with water, and draw the corners up to meet over each apple.

7 Press the edges of the dough firmly together and decorate with dough leaves and shapes made from the extra dough trimmings.

8 Place the apples on the prepared cookie sheet, brush with the egg white, and sprinkle with the sugar.

9 Bake in the preheated oven for 30 minutes or until golden and the crust and apples are cooked. Serve the dumplings hot with the custard sauce or vanilla sauce.

2

6

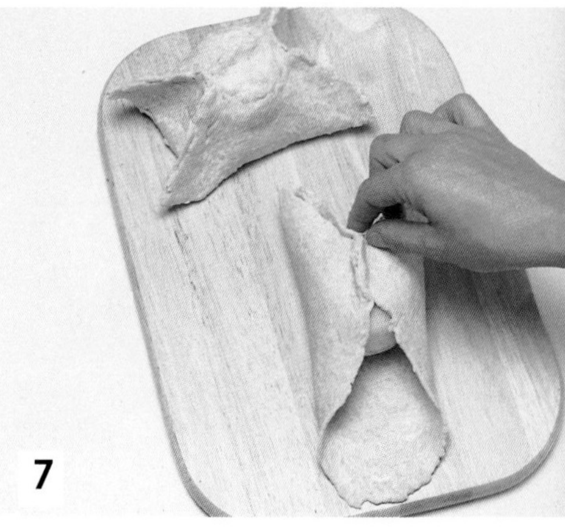
7

Jam Roly Poly

INGREDIENTS

Serves 6

2 cups/$\frac{1}{2}$ lb self-rising flour
$\frac{1}{4}$ tsp salt
$\frac{1}{2}$ cup/$\frac{1}{4}$ lb shredded suet
$\frac{2}{3}$ cup/$\frac{1}{4}$ pint water
3 tbsp strawberry jelly
1 tbsp milk, to glaze
1 tsp superfine sugar
ready-made jelly sauce, to serve

TASTY TIP

To make jelly sauce, warm 4 tablespoons jelly, such as seedless raspberry jelly, with $\frac{2}{3}$ cup/$\frac{1}{4}$ pint water or orange juice. Stir until smooth. Blend 2 teaspoons arrowroot with 1 tablespoon water or juice to a smooth paste. Bring the jelly mixture to almost boiling point, then stir in the blended arrowroot. Cook, stirring until the mixture thickens slightly and clears, then serve.

1 Preheat the oven to 400°F. Make the dough by sifting the flour and salt into a large bowl.

2 Add the suet and mix lightly, then add the water a little at a time and mix to form a soft and pliable dough. (Take care not to make the dough too wet.)

3 Turn the dough out onto a lightly floured board and knead gently until smooth.

4 Roll the dough out into a 9 x 11-inch rectangle.

5 Spread the jelly over the dough leaving a border of $\frac{1}{2}$ inch all around. Fold the border over the jelly and brush the edges with water.

6 Lightly roll the rectangle up from one of the short sides, seal the top edge, and press the ends together. (Do not roll the dessert up too tightly.)

7 Turn the dessert upside down onto a large piece of greased baking parchment large enough to come halfway up the sides.

8 Tie the ends of the paper, to make a boat-shaped paper case for the dessert to sit in and to leave plenty of room for the roly poly to expand.

9 Brush the dessert lightly with milk and sprinkle with the sugar. Bake in the preheated oven for 30–40 minutes, or until well risen and golden. Serve immediately with the jelly sauce.

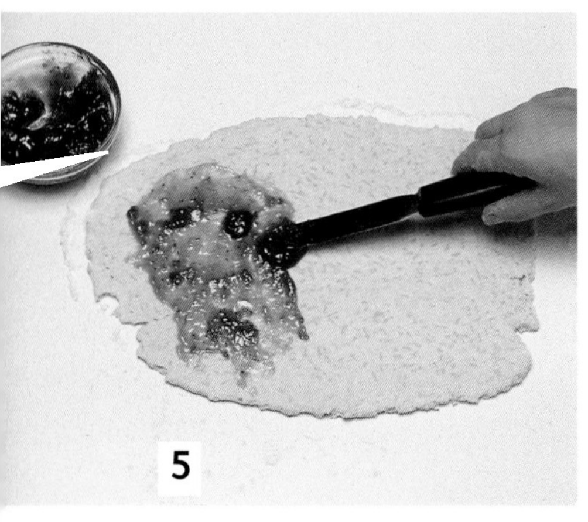
5

6

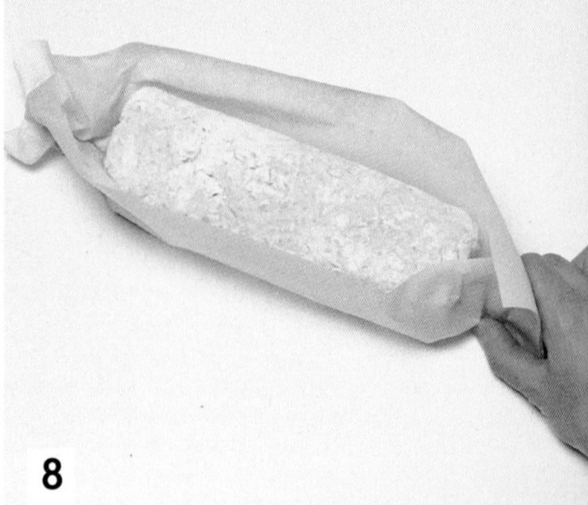
8

Egg Custard Tart

INGREDIENTS

Serves 6

For the sweet pie crust:

1/2 stick/2 oz butter

4 tbsp/2 oz shortening

1 1/2 cups/6 oz all-purpose flour

1 egg yolk, beaten

2 tsp superfine sugar

For the filling:

1 1/4 cups/1/2 pint milk

2 eggs, plus 1 egg yolk

2 tbsp/1 oz superfine sugar

1/2 tsp nutmeg, freshly grated

HELPFUL HINT

Nowadays eggs are normally date stamped so it is possible to be sure that they are eaten when they are at their best. Another way to test if an egg is fresh is to place an uncooked egg in a bowl of water—if it lies at the bottom it is fresh; if it tilts it is older (use for frying or scrambling); if it floats, discard.

1. Preheat the oven to 400°F. Grease an 8-inch flan pan or dish.
2. Make the dough by cutting the butter and shortening into small cubes. Add to the flour in a large bowl and rub in, until the mixture resembles fine bread crumbs.
3. Add the egg, sugar, and enough water to form a soft and pliable dough. Turn onto a lightly floured board and knead. Wrap and chill in the refrigerator for 30 minutes.
4. Roll the dough out onto a lightly floured surface or board and use to line the greased flan pan. Place in the refrigerator to chill.
5. Warm the milk in a small saucepan. Briskly beat together the eggs, egg yolk, and superfine sugar.
6. Pour the milk into the egg mixture and beat until blended.
7. Strain through a strainer into the tart shell. Place the flan pan on a cookie sheet.
8. Sprinkle the top of the tart with nutmeg and bake in the preheated oven for about 15 minutes.
9. Turn the oven down to 325°F and bake for a further 30 minutes, or until the custard has set. Serve hot or cold.

2

5

7

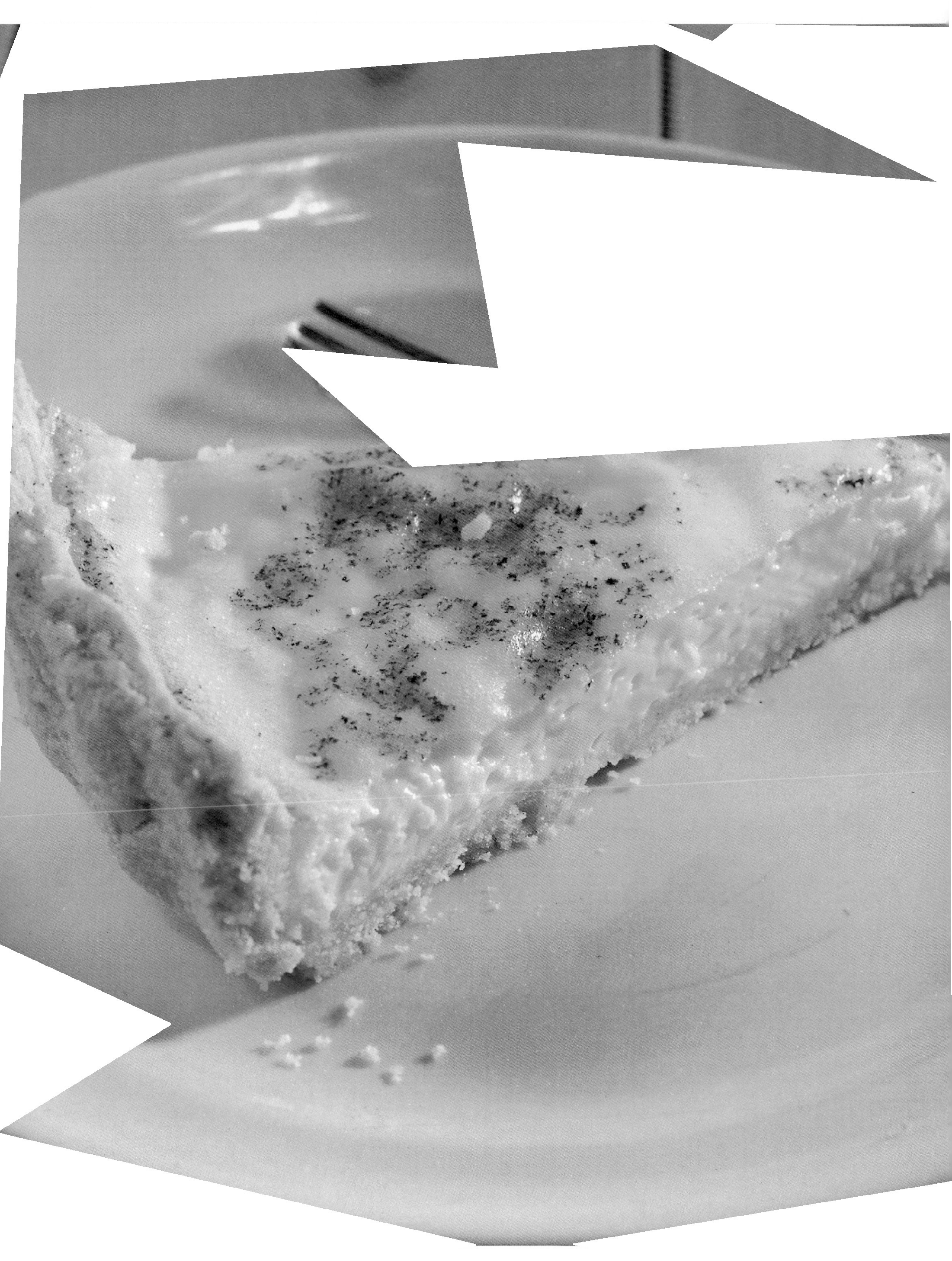

Index